TALES FROM THE
PALOUSE COUNTRY

Robert Easton

TALES FROM THE
PALOUSE COUNTRY

ReadersMagnet, LLC

Tales from the Palouse Country
Copyright © 2019 by Robert Easton

Published in the United States of America
ISBN Paperback: 978-1-950947-36-2
ISBN eBook: 978-1-950947-37-9

All rights reserved. No part of this publication may be reproduced, stored in a retrieval system or transmitted in any way by any means, electronic, mechanical, photocopy, recording or otherwise without the prior permission of the author except as provided by USA copyright law.

The opinions expressed by the author are not necessarily those of ReadersMagnet, LLC.

ReadersMagnet, LLC
10620 Treena Street, Suite 230 | San Diego, California, 92131 USA
1.619.354.2643 | www.readersmagnet.com

Book design copyright © 2019 by ReadersMagnet, LLC. All rights reserved.
Cover design by Ericka Walker
Interior design by Shemaryl Evans

DEDICATION

Because many of the books published today are written by and about "big name" celebrities, I dedicate this book to the millions of struggling, dreaming unknowns like myself; the unestablished part-time beginning writers, the talented small-press people, the persevering editors of literary magazines, and last but not least, my family, without whose patience, support, and understanding this book would not have become a reality.

The Author

ACKNOWLEDGEMENTS

Many thanks to the Battle Days Association Committee (whoever they are) and to the unknown author of "On The Battleground" from whose booklets I have extracted passages.

Also thanks to The Tower Press, Inc., Seabrook, New Hampshire, for publishing the third and fourth chapters of this book as short articles in "Good Old Days" magazine under the titles, "Magic Moments" and "Kite Flying Days ", respectively.

Finally, thanks to Hibiscus Press (In A Nutshell), Sacramento, California, for publishing "The Maiden Flight of The Windsocket".

The Author

INTRODUCTION

The following pages contain exaggerated essays concerning my experiences growing up in a small town in "The Palouse Country" of eastern Washington Stale.

All of the "tales"—are based on actual incidents but some of the names of places and people have been changed or deleted to protect the guilty—and the innocent! For that reason the town remains nameless but some readers will probably recognize it immediately. For those that don't, hopefully they will identify it as typical of a small wheat town.

Some of the stories are nostalgic satires. Others are "fictionalized fact" or "factualized fiction", whichever the reader prefers. Some are the wordy, rambling kinds of yarns that have traditionally been spun around pot-bellied stoves in barbershops, pool halls and the backrooms of country stores.

Certain pertinent dates and facts come from the pages of a diary I kept during that relatively uneventful time between the end of the Second World War and the beginning of the Korean conflict. Much of the material is drawn purely from my childhood memories of the late 1930's and early 1940's.

All of the "tales" have settings in the Palouse (pronounced Pa-loose) with the exception of "Horse Tales", in which a portion involves the Okanogan Highlands. However, in all of the stories,

I've tried to not only give them some of the charm and "flavor" of the Palouse but also some "universal" appeal.

Therefore, they are not in any sense, straight non-fiction nor are they experimental, mainstream fiction, pure nostalgia or what has come to be known as "Americana".

The fertile Palouse hills are rolling vast wheat lands over 3000 square miles in an area from which billions of dollars' worth of grain has been produced and sent all over the world. Recently, with the addition of commercial fertilizers, the yield per acre has increased immensely.

Despite all this, and even though Palouse farms are larger, the region has been frequently confused with the wheat-growing midwestern states. Both areas have been referred to as the "breadbasket of the world".

I have described the region only superficially as it applies to the material. That is, I have not given annual rainfall rates, temperatures, bushels per acre, and many other statistics. I consider myself a creative writer, not a repeater of known truths, and books have already been written giving the historic, geographic, and geologic facts about the area.

Other non-fiction works have dealt with early explorations and discoveries, the Indian inhabitants, the missionaries, the fur traders, and the early pioneers and settlers.

Fascinated by my own memories, experience, and imagination, I felt compelled to write these narratives because to my knowledge this is the only work of its kind ever written by a native son about the Palouse hills during that time period.

With the possible exceptions of Grand Coulee Dam, the Columbia Basin Project, and the recent Expo 74 in Spokane, most articles and stories of major note to come out of Washington State have been written by, for and about the residents of western Washington.

The "scenic" tourist spots around Seattle, Tacoma, the Olympic rainforest, and the Cascade Range have enjoyed much publicity but the lesser populated wheat country has been definitely slighted.

Much of the material is confessional in nature and necessarily tied together with bits of autobiography.

Some of my characters are composites of country people I've met during the course of my life and some of the incidents, likewise, are merely fabrication built upon half truths.

The reader must understand that the material concerning my boyhood, especially my infancy, was seen through my eyes only and therefore may be erroneous and incomplete. No doubt many of my contemporaries will disagree with my text but the human mind has its limitations. Parts of the contents may be redundant and insignificant while perhaps some of the truly important "happenings" may have been omitted altogether.

If some of these reminiscences seem like pure fantasy, I'm genuinely sorry but any writer knows it is extremely difficult to be objective about one's life and times.

The observations and commentary known today as "author intrusion" are those of a country bumpkin trying to adjust to urban life. Therefore, it should be obvious to the reader that "you can take the boy out of the country but you can't take the country out of the boy".

So this book is many books. It is a collection of tall tales: an autobiography, a confession, and an incomplete history of a family, a town, a region, and an era.

In an age when we all hearken back to the "good old days," wanting to believe they were actually better because of the traumas of the present, it is my wish that the reader find these stories refreshingly different.

THE AUTHOR
WHERE IS THE PALOUSE?

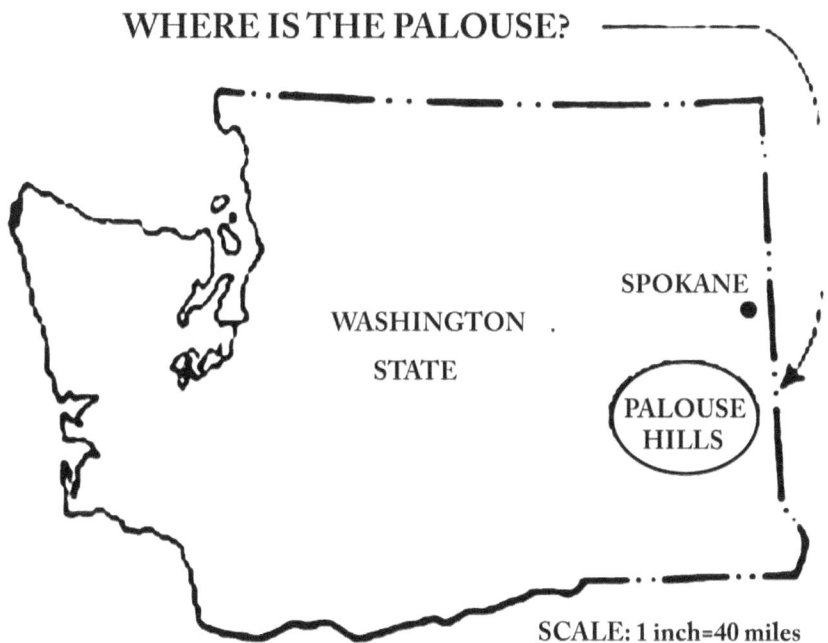

CONTENTS

CHAPTER ONE: Dead Soldiers In The Cheat Grass 1
CHAPTER TWO: The Great Bank Robbery
                And Other Memories 9
CHAPTER THREE: The Great Virgil 23
CHAPTER FOUR: The Maiden Flight Of The Windsocket 31
CHAPTER FIVE: Horse Tales 39
CHAPTER SIX: The Gentle Art 51
CHAPTER SEVEN: Summers With The Gandies 59
CHAPTER EIGHT: A Random Harvest 73
CHAPTER NINE: Funny Norman And The Mouse Game 83
CHAPTER TEN: Killsport 93
CHAPTER ELEVEN: Miscellaneous Unrelated Incidents
                And Comments 103
CHAPTER TWELVE: The Divine Flora 117
CHAPTER THIRTEEN: The End Of The Beginning 123

THE AUTHOR 131

CHAPTER ONE

DEAD SOLDIERS IN THE CHEAT GRASS

In the summer of 1976 I went back to the town in which I spent most of the first 18 years of my life.

I had been away a long time and it seemed fitting during that bicentennial summer to make that sentimental journey to better understand and appreciate the nature of my origins.

It was not an experience unique to mankind. People are always going back to somewhere; their birthplaces, their old city neighborhoods, or their class reunions in their hometowns.

But what makes them do this? Because they want to see how things have changed? To relive past glories? To try to recapture the sweet bird of youth? To gloat with superiority? To right old wrongs? To discover from the past new paths to a better future? Or for a thousand other reasons?

Out of my mixed feelings of nostalgia, humility, joy, curiosity and dread the idea for this collection of memories, essays, and tales was born.

I drove into town that day in late June via Cheney, Pine City, and Malden to find my town was not at all the ghost town I was expecting. In fact it had outlived most of the others in the area and was prospering.

The town had grown but little in population but perhaps the reason for its survival at all was because a new freeway replaced the old Inland

Empire highway. And also because of the hamlet's distinction of being the site of an Indian skirmish, much to the delight of eastern Washington State historians.

Therefore I drove first to the Monument on the hill. I couldn't help noticing how manicured it looked, so unlike the way I remembered it. In the back to the east were shiny painted restrooms and I couldn't remember any being there before.

So as I stood there at the Monument I wondered why I came back. The circumstances under which I left will help the reader better understand my feelings upon returning. These circumstances are explained in part on the following pages.

As far back as the middle 1930's my brother and I would go to the top of one of the highest hills on the outskirts of town to visit that old Monument. Next to a wheat field on a southwest point, it seemed less than an acre in size and surrounded by a barbwire fence.

As I recall, a dirt road or perhaps just a path led out of town at a winding angle along a fence through fields up to the Monument's entrance. Over that entrance was a crude arch bearing a sign and the name of the sign's maker, neither of which I remember.

Inside, enclosed by a black wrought-iron fence, was a tall, spear-shaped shaft of granite, a smaller version of the one in Washington. D.C.

We called it and the space it occupied The Steptoe Monument.

Engraved in the granite on the west face are the words, "In memory of the officers and soldiers of the United States Army who lost their lives on this field in desperate conflict with the Indians in the battle of Te-Hots-Nim-Me May 17, 1858."

The south face reads:

> Killed in Conflict
> Capt. O.H.P. Taylor
> Sargt. Wm. G. Williams
> Alfred Barnes
> Victor Chas. DeMoy

> James Crozet
> Charles H. Harnish
>
> ---
>
> All of the first dragoons
>   United States Army

On the north face is:

> In memory of Chief Tam-Mv-Tsa
>   (Timothy)
> and the Nez Perces Christian Indians
> Rescuers of the Steptoe Expedition

And finally, the east face reads:

> Erected by
> Esther Reed Chapter
> Daughters of the American Revolution
> Spokane, Wash.
> June 14. 1914

By anyone's standards, the Monument at that time (1930's) was poorly maintained because the fence posts were rotted off and leaning. The barbwire was hanging loose. Weeds were everywhere.

The worst weed, though, was cheatgrass, the Scourge of the West. To try and walk through the stuff wearing low shoes is foolhardy because soon the tiny spears have filled both socks and shoes and scratch the wearer's feet and legs to such an uncomfortable extent it is possible madness can result.

This weed is found in great abundance throughout the Palouse along with Burdock (cockleburrs), nettles, Russian thistle, Canadian thistle, and tansy. I shall discuss tansy at greater length in a following chapter but suffice it to say I think all of the above plants thrived in the Monument.

Anyway, we kids grew up without really grasping the significance of the history behind the marker so I grew up believing the following: A band of U.S. Cavalrymen fleeing hostile Indians tried to make a stand on that hill above town. The white men, I was told, were led by Colonel Steptoe who was a lot like General Custer and soon found himself surrounded by Indians.

However, either reinforcements arrived or the Indians got tired because Steptoe and some of his men escaped to make another stand further south on what is now called Steptoe Butte, a large hill standing out like a sore thumb in the midst of all that flat land.

Our parents told us that it was on the Monument site where a number of white soldiers fell and small oval bronze markers were placed giving the name and other data about each soldier buried there. Later research failed to turn up any information about the markers so I don't know what happened to them. Maybe I dreamed of them. No markers were made for the Indians. Either none were killed or the coyotes got their remains.

As I've written, we kids were too young to appreciate this little tidbit of history and maybe only an idiot would try to recall it now.

However, the Battle Days Association Committee gives this account of the skirmish:

> "On May 8, 1958, Col. Steptoe and 157 officers and men, about 30 civilians, several Indian scouts and a pack train of 85 pack animals, left Fort Walla Walla on an armed expedition into the country north of the Snake River. After a leisurely march of 8 days, they encountered hostile Indians a few miles north of (my home town). They camped on the night of May 16th at the junction of Babb and the Cheney road and started a retreat the next morning. Steptoe had made the decision to retreat because the soldiers were outnumbered and the Indians had better weapons, and also because most of the spare ammunition had been left in Ft. Walla Walla.
>
> After a running fight over the hills north of town, they retreated to the hill east of (my home town), where the Steptoe Battle Monument now stands.
>
> They stood off the Indians until dark and were then led through an unguarded section of the enemy lines by Chief Timothy, a Nez Perce scout and made a headlong flight to Ft. Walla Walla. Seven soldiers, one civilian and several friendly Indians had been killed in the engagement."

This account raises some questions about why the spare ammunition was left, who the civilian was as well as who were the friendly Indians and what happened to their bodies? Also it implies that Steptoe may have been a little like Custer at that.

Excerpts from a book entitled. "On The Battleground" written by an unknown author, reveal a somewhat closer look at what happened:

> "At dusk of May 18, 1858, thirty miles south, as the crow flies, from the falls of Spokane River, the Steptoe Expedition halted and prepared to make its last stand. Crazed with blood and victory, thousands of painted savages, gathered from the Yakimas to the Coeur d' Alenes, hung like wolves to flanks, front and rear.
>
> The command had reached the bend where Pine creek turns directly eastward. Here the ridge along which they had battled since mid-day ends abruptly in steep descents to Pine creek to south and west. At this place the valley narrows to a few hundred yards, the opposite side of the stream rising in a precipitous bluff. On this favored ground for defense the troops were halted and prepared to withstand the expected night attack as best they could.
>
> Several days of fierce fighting left them with not five rounds of ammunition and depressed by the loss of comrades and two most trusted officers, an inevitable massacre seemed the fate of the morrow.
>
> At a hasty council, called by Colonel Steptoe, it was decided that their only hope was to leave all baggage and steal or cut their way through the cordon of the enemy. Scouts were sent out and it was discovered that the bluff directly opposite was unguarded. The Indians believed it too precipitous for the soldiers to mount. It was determined to scale it. Everything that impeded flight-tents, pack animals and supplies was abandoned. During the halt, three of the wounded-mortally hurt-mercifully died, either by the will of Providence or because of those dark compacts that existed in the days of Indian warfare, never to let a wounded comrade fall alive into the hands of torturing foes.

The howitzers were dismounted, the gun carriages sunk in Pine Creek and the cannon buried with the remains of Captain Taylor. Their horses were then led to and fro over the spot to remove all traces of interment.

At midnight, all preparation made, they silently deserted the obliterated graves of comrades and beloved captain. He had been spared the tale of defeat and flight which brave men do not care to survive to tell.

THE ESCAPE

W*ITH HOOFS MUFFLED, HUSHING THE* moans *of the wounded, the soldiers stealthily led their horses across the ford and successfully clambered up the steep bluffs undiscovered. They then mounted, and at daybreak, when the Indians charged the deserted camp, twelve miles away they were passing the base of that grand pyramid, which rising high, towers like a mighty sentinel silently watching over the thousand Palouse hills, and which to this day bears the name of Steptoe Butte."*

There have been countless versions written about the battle and probably none of them are completely accurate. The biggest error, however. seems to be in the number of Indians on the scene. Certainly there were not "thousands of painted savages".

The Spokane Indians were the largest group in the vicinity but they may not have even fought. The Couer d' Alenes may have numbered 400 but 100 were females. Two warriors were killed in the battle and one died later of wounds. The Palouse were a small group and there were no more than 20 Nez Perce which were used as guides. Timothy, who was about 58 years old at the time, may not even have been with them, let alone led the rescuers.

The Indian side of the story is vague but one incident involved a Cayuse Indian named Wycat (spelling?) who was used by the white men as a scout and messenger. It seems Wycat was sent for help and performed a remarkable feat of horsemanship by traveling 250 miles in two days down the rugged Snake River canyon.

Part of this trip must have been made in the dark and more than one horse may have been used. Of course at that time there were wild horses on the ranges which he might have ridden. It seems that in the early times, Spanish adventurers brought horses to North America. The descendants of some of these animals were probably Mustangs. But the Nez Perce Indians of Idaho and Washington in the meantime were developing a unique dapple-bottomed critter throughout the Palouse River region. Hence the name Appaloosa comes from the word Palouse.

Anyway, the Indians surrendered in September of 1858 and Wycat was hanged by Wright sometime later, according to regional history.

Unappreciative of all this Indian lore, my brother and I would either walk or ride our bicycles to the Monument in the spring and summer months for a variety of other reasons.

Often we'd go to sit in the shade of the chestnut trees and gather the nuts (also called buckeyes) we found scattered beneath them. We'd use the nuts to make toy pipes and other doodads. Sometimes we'd take our .22 caliber rifles and shoot at ground squirrels and an occasional rabbit.

Every kid in town must have had some sort of rifle because the grave markers had plenty of holes in them.

We did find a few arrowheads and somebody in town found a spearhead as I recall. It's now in the Spokane County Museum, I suppose. Along with that field cannon somebody was rumored to have found in the creek on the west side of town.

I don't know what my brother did with his arrowheads but I kept mine in a little box along with my Boy Scout badges and other boyish treasures.

I haven't cleaned out the garage for a long time but the next time I do I plan to search again for that little box with Indian history in it.

As we grew older, some of we high schoolers used the Monument for a "lover's lane". The gate was never locked and the place afforded a lot of seclusion for private nocturnal activities. What amorous adventures must have gone unobserved over the years in the shadow of that phallic pinnacle! I spent a few Saturday nights up there myself with this girl Jeannie but more about her will follow in later chapters.

The Monument was also a great spot for beer drinking because it was such a handy place for the guys to throw their "dead soldiers" (empty beer bottles) into the cheat grass.

CHAPTER TWO

THE GREAT BANK ROBBERY AND OTHER MEMORIES

Our town was named after the wife of the first settler and along with those Indians and the misadventures of Colonel Steptoe, the town's only other claim to fame was the Great Bank Robbery in 1935.

Not everybody in town could recall the settlers or the Indians because that was ancient history to a lot of us. But everybody knew about the Great Bank Robbery because it was recent history and all us kids had looked at the bullet holes in the bricks of the bank building lots of times.

I recall dad and mom telling us all about what happened. I can remember they said that the town marshall had been killed. The robbers, who cleverly started a fire in a house in the south end of town as a diversion, had it all planned out.

All the deputies, firemen and townspeople were at the fire when the robbers made their move but the marshall was suspicious that something was amiss and these suspicions led to his death. Dad said the marshall doubled back to town and was shot in the back by a man dressed as a woman sitting in the back seat of the getaway car which was parked beside the bank.

Through the years there have been many versions of the incident but the following account was written in 1966 by the bank manager who was taken hostage:

> "In August, 1935, three thugs moved in on us at 3:00 one afternoon. We normally closed at 4:00 o'clock and the closing one hour early is what called attention to the holdup.
>
> During the holdup the town marshall was killed by the driver of the getaway car as he was firing through the front window at the thugs inside. He was shot in the back with buckshot. His name was _____ and he was a good friend of mine and well liked by most persons in the area. The F.B.I. finally picked up one of the bandits, but the others were never caught as far as I know. The one who was caught is still serving the three life sentences he picked up that afternoon for murder, bank robbery, and kidnapping, plus one he was serving for murder from which he had escaped prison prior to the robbery.
>
> I was the one who was kidnapped. They took me about two or three miles toward Spokane from (my hometown) and without slowing down ordered me to jump. I didn't care for their company anyway, and since they went well in authority, I jumped. I hitch-hiked back to (my hometown) and called all the sheriff's offices, etc., in a complete ring around the area, in an attempt to cut them off."

So much for the bank robbery story, because as far as I'm concerned this book begins right here with memories of my life that go as far back as I can remember.

In 1931 I was born in Prosser in the Horse Heaven hills of Central Washington State. My father was a hired hand on chicken ranches and even though he had attended college, times were tough and after he met my mother in college and married her, about the only work he could get was either picking fruit or working on those chicken ranches.

From Prosser, our parents moved to Colfax to another chicken ranch and from there soon to the outskirts of my hometown and that's how we kids came to live in such a God-forsaken wilderness in the first place.

I remember dad describing to me the trip north from Colfax in that old truck that must have looked like the Joad family coming from Oklahoma with all us kids piled in among that rickety furniture.

Dad said his boss had this German Shepherd police dog named King who ran behind the truck the entire 28 miles until we got to our new home which was just a lot of barns called Freshlaid Farms.

Yes, just a group of barns a couple miles south of town and I lived there with my older sister and younger brother when we were all just toddlers. A house had been built into one end of one of the biggest barns and when we opened the back door, there was a haymow!

Dad's job was to feed, water, and otherwise take care of thousands of White Leghorns, Rhode Island Reds, Plymouth Rocks and even some turkeys and geese which were all in different stages of development and housed in long red chickenhouses. The big boss even had some horses and dairy cows roaming around which as I recall were so anemic they gave blue milk.

One of my first memories was of being awakened one hot afternoon by a big horse fly which kept buzzing around my face. My brother lay asleep beside me, no adults in sight.

I woke him; we both tore off our clothes and for some unknown reason, ran naked out the back door, down between two long chickenhouses, hopping over fresh cowpies as we ran under that fierce summer sun.

A couple of hired hands saw us and grinned at each other. Then one yelled at us, "Hey, where's the race?"

The chicken ranch was surrounded on three sides by wheat fields and the waving grain in the springtime was like a sweet-smelling ocean. By August, it had turned golden brown and the roads and paths around the outbuildings were dusty. We had no lawn.

When the combines moved in to harvest, there were choking clouds of dust and it was during one of those summers just before the harvest when the wheat was at its highest, my sister got lost in all that grain. It was an easy thing for a kid to do and we were lucky to find her. She emerged tired, scared and very thirsty.

The bits and pieces of memories come back to me now like a series of sketches on an artist's pad. I remember the nanny goat and her kids we had that would butt us off the front porch when we were just two ragged little barefoot boys in bib overalls.

I remember dad telling of the night he went into the barn after we had just been given King for protection and the dog leaped for his throat. Dad said he jumped aside just in time, shouted the dog's name and held the flashlight off to one side.

All this reminds me of a lot of other pets we had too. Lots of cats but mostly dogs; Australian Shepherds, Collies, and later Cocker Spaniels. I remember Lady was the first and smartest of our shepherds. Then there were the collies, Lad and Lassie, the cockers, Susie and Kilroy, and eventually Trixie, the Boston bull terrier.

We would take rides around the countryside on Sunday afternoons in dad's old Whippet and later, the Rockney. I recall leaving a toy ivory elephant on the running board of one of those cars. The elephant was a Crackerjack box prize and I cried so much dad and I retraced the route all the way back to town without ever finding it.

I remember walking up the lane to visit the old couple named Ruebel with the heavy European accents who used to sit us on their laps and give us milk and homemade filling cookies with raisins and nuts in them.

My first days of school were not happy ones and my sister had been taking me with her every morning to get me used to it but one day she was sick and I had to make the walk alone. I walked up the long flight of cement steps to the entrance but some girl kept swinging her lunch pail and shouting at me. I got so scared I went back home and refused to leave the house that day.

I remember walking across that big cement overpass with my brother on our way to school a year later and having to stop and hang onto the bridge when big trucks or buses passed to avoid being sucked under the wheels.

I remember the winters when dad carried me to school the one mile on his shoulders with the drifts piled high above our heads on both sides of the road. I guess we didn't live far enough away to be eligible for a school bus ride.

It was during one of these severe winters that I recall getting my foot caught under a barrel of water on a sled and losing my big toenail.

The highlight of the first grade was playing the part of Bashful in Snow White and The Seven Dwarfs. About this time I must have learned how to read and entered the fascinating world of comic books and indulged my fancy in the likes of characters like Smilin Jack, Tailspin Tommy, Terry and The Pirates, and Cap'n Easy.

Soon I was reading and trading not only comic books but big-little books and all kinds of men's magazines. However, I lived in such isolation my trading had to be done at school. So far all my reading material had pictures in it and I hadn't yet discovered the library which existed on the other side of town but may as well have been on the moon.

Eventually we moved from the barn into town to the house on the hill and the top of a long flight of 52 wooden stairs where we could look down on the roof of the Christian Church.

Dad left Freshlaid Farms and got a job as night marshall for sixty dollars a month.

That was in the early 1930's when the country was just pulling out of the Depression and jobs were still scarce but that job was ridiculous! Here was a man with three little kids and a wife trying to hold down a night job and sleep in the daytime! Fat chance! Little boys are too noisy for that!

My brother and I used to slip into dad's bedroom when he was asleep and play with his nightstick and blackjack which he called a "sap". We also played with the handcuffs and even his revolver too, all lying there on the dresser. It's a miracle we didn't kill ourselves.

I remember that day after Christmas when with our new pocketknives we were stabbing pictures of sexy-looking girls in magazines. My brother got his wrist in the way and my knife stabbed the back of his hand. His screams woke dad and he came tearing out in his pajamas a frightful figure to behold and so mad he was livid. He pressed his hands on my brother's artery to stop the blood flow, dressed the wound and went back to bed.

Dad never talked much about his job and he lived in his own private world. That was understandable because how can the duties of a law enforcement officer he explained to three little children?

He would make a remark or two now and then about checking doors and sort of walking guard duty. I do recall him telling us about some drunk coming at him one night in the tavern determined to kill him with a piece of two by four. We kids never heard the details about that incident.

I don't really know all he did as a town marshall but I know he saw the worst of people and the worst in people. He must have worked with other policemen and the county sheriff but he never talked about it. I do know he didn't want my brother and I to be "street roamers", hanging around the streets at night like some other smart-alecky kids he would send home sometimes.

Life must have been hell in those days for dad but how well we remember that wintry night while making his rounds checking shop doors he found Trixie. Only that wasn't her name then. She was just a half-frozen Boston bull terrier pup, the smartest dog we ever had.

She could roll over, sit up. beg for food, speak, and in the country on outings, all we had to do was blow the car horn and she'd be there.

Trixie was a living example of why people who abandon animals to starve and freeze to death should be fined or sent to prison or both.

One of my first conscious memories of grade school was that blizzardy day when school was dismissed at noon because the boiler had overheated and the custodian was afraid it was going to explode.

Another vivid, bittersweet impression from those years was my first love, little Nancy Dietler, with her blonde curls who sat in front of me in the fifth grade. How I wished I hadn't dunked her curls in the inkwell! She slapped my face and that ended our relationship but I know now she hardly even knew I was alive anyway. She was hopelessly in love with Chuck Smollet at the time.

I remember how the sixth grade class roared with laughter the following year during social studies when some kid was reading aloud about all the "brassieres ' in Africa. Of course we knew this was incorrect as well as the fact the word he couldn't pronounce was "bazaars". Since the kid had two older sisters, we were willing to believe it was an honest mistake.

There were only two times in my young life when I really felt anger, the kind of white-hot rage that can turn a peaceful person into a murderer.

The first time was in the third grade when our 300 pound teacher. Miss Weston, was reading the "Five Little Peppers and How They Grew" aloud to the class. I was following along with my own library copy of the book and the retard named Billy Watts who sat behind me was a poor reader and kept snapping my suspenders because he wanted me to give him the book so he could follow along.

He kept snapping those suspenders harder and harder until the pain got really intense. I should have given him the book because it might have helped him learn some new words but I didn't and finally got so mad I turned around and slammed the book down on the top of his head.

I ran up the aisle with him chasing me and buried my face right in that fat teacher's skirts. Startled though she was, she kept that bully from killing me but he did chase me all the way home from school that night.

The second time was when I was in high school and it happened in the gymnasium at Oaksdale one snowy night during a basketball game. Some drunken belligerent kid, who never should have been allowed admittance in the first place, was looking for a fight.

Everybody ignored him including me but when he pushed a friend of mine over the bleachers onto the floor I became enraged and told the kid I'd fight him. With him were two big, plug-uglies wearing leather jackets and helping the kid stay on his feet. I figured the one that looked like Marlon Brando would probably kill me after I dispatched the drunk but I was so mad! I didn't care.

I just jerked the kid down from the balcony and outside in front of the big doors and prepared to do battle. The guy in the ticket window was pretending not to see the whole thing.

It was snowing hard as I brought my fist back to smash the punk but as the two mugs let loose the kid fell into my arms out cold. His breath was strong enough to knock out an ox. And I never even got a chance to hit him. I was frustrated but the others just carried the kid away and I went back inside to watch the game.

Looking back, I remember my sister dressing my brother and I up like Indians for some kind of neighborhood play. She put towels on us for breech clouts and feathers in our hair.

Later, one twilight. my brother and I performed as drunken clowns for the neighboring housewives. The act consisted mostly of the two of us walking along the board sidewalk, stumbling and falling down to reveal holes in the seats of our pants. We purposely were not wearing underwear.

My world was small then but I do recall some trips. Like dad's annual pilgrimage down to Penawawa on the Snake River to pick fruit. I'll never know how our old cars made that dusty trip but I do remember looking up in that apricot tree and seeing a gigantic bull snake over my head.

Among my earliest recollections of the early Thirties was of all us kids piling into the car and going to Grandma's house in the country near Cheney.

The trip was made over gravel and dirt roads usually on some family reunion occasion or Thanksgiving. Sometimes we made the trip in the rain and once we kids all bumped our heads on the car roof after going into the ditch. Dad had been driving into a blinding sunset and was forced off the road by a car coming in the opposite direction.

Grandpa's farm was exciting because it was different. He had an apple orchard and a cider press on which a cousin of ours cut off the top half of the middle finger of his left hand.

With regret I also look back and remember throwing a rotten apple and killing a red-headed woodpecker that was trying to live peacefully in that orchard.

The farm was about 40 acres. I believe, and today it would be called "diversified" because Grandpa raised grain crops, melons, fruits, and all kinds of vegetables including some unusual items like dill for pickles.

At the reunions, the grownups would mostly just eat and talk while we kids fooled around outside in the barn and outbuildings playing Hide-and-Seek, Kick-the-Can, or Red Rover, Come Over. Dad was from a large family (10) so I had many aunts, uncles, and cousins, some of them seen so infrequently I hardly knew them.

We were just tots so sometimes several of us were all deposited in the same bed and we must have gone to bed early because in the winter it got dark as soon as the sun went down and Grandpa had to bring out those smoky, smelly old kerosene lanterns.

There was no indoor plumbing and the outhouse was quite a distance from our upstairs bedroom. It was spooky going down those dark stairs with Grandma or Grandpa out to that shadowy old cube with the half-moon in it. I do remember later that Grandma put chamber pots in the room for my brother and I which helped considerably but they were tricky to use while standing there shaking from the cold. I could have predicted the demise of the outhouse and yet its value was in helping mankind appreciate creature comforts. Natural man may one day return to its charms.

All this time I was still dreaming about how it would be when I was a man and wanted desperately to leave this small town in favor of big city lights. I thought the path of real Adventure led to New York, London, or Paris and wanted to be either a private detective or a foreign war correspondent. Meanwhile, I read lots of books and built model airplanes from cutouts on the backs of Wheaties packages.

But what I really remember on those occasions at Grandma's house was lying awake at night beside my brother and hearing the mournful whistle of an outward bound freight somewhere in the scrub timber west of Cheney. It sure gave me an awful restless wanderlust.

Maybe all kids love to be scared and we were no exception. That's why we'd spend a lot of time sitting around telling ghost stories. With all the reading I'd done and after listening to The Shadow, I Love a Mystery, and Inner Sanctum on the radio, I was an eager participant.

A good time to tell them was either just before or after Halloween or on some dark night following a snipe hunt. A couple of incidents had happened in town to really add fuel to these tales, the first being that time a man hanged himself in the barn behind our house thus giving us nightmares for a long time after.

I had a low threshold of courage because I remember running all the way home one bright afternoon after seeing the matinee performance of "Snow White and the Seven Dwarfs" at the movie house. That witch really terrified me. I also had nightmares after my brother and I caught a bunch of crawdads and buried them alive in the back yard. In my dreams, they grew to enormous size and crawled out to take over the town.

Also, our friends were all older kids who thrilled at the idea of either teasing us to madness or scaring our brains out with some harebrained yarn.

Anyway, one Halloween after all the pranks had been played, like soaping windows and running those empty notched thread spools across old people's windows, we decided to have a story contest.

A prize was to be given to the one who could tell the best ghost story. Now we all knew that the setting had to be right for such an event and somebody's room was just not scary enough.

I'll never know why we didn't go to the cemetery on the north edge of town because it was rumored that graves were sometimes left open or were sunken in and that ghosts had been heard and seen out there.

Finally, we decided to meet beneath the old concrete railroad bridge south of town at midnight. Naturally, the night was dark despite the light from a somber moon.

My brother and I climbed out our bedroom window, trudged down the railroad tracks to the meeting place and the shadows and noises seemed all around us. The telegraph poles cast shadows fifty feet tall which moved like giant's fingers to grab us at every turn.

Grade school kids can have vivid imaginations and by the time we reached the rendezvous, we were susceptible to any kind of supernatural fantasy that might be presented. In other words, we were shaking in our boots.

The stories started with the most simple, dull, and overused ghost tales but soon progressed to some terrifying suspense stories not too unlike those of Edgar Allen Poe or H. Rider Haggard.

The story that won the contest and had us all screaming and running home, however, was narrated by the kid who told us about the bridge we were sitting under. Later, we realized he was the one that had decided on the contest location.

According to him, a workman had fallen into the cement mixer when the bridge was built and the body was never recovered. With candles and a cheap flashlight, the kid told us he was going to show us where the body was because the man's face was still visible on the surface of one of the bridge abutments.

Needless to say, none of us cared to stick around to see the proof.

And all this happened just after that new girl and her folks from Montana moved into town.

They moved into the old Boardman house, a castle-like structure just a few blocks south of us. From the brow of the hill my brother and I could look down on the top of that huge palace.

But the girl was as impressive as the house. With her black hair and eyes and with those long dark lashes, she was a real beauty and very exciting to us because she was sort of flirty. Also, not too many new people ever came to town and stayed.

Quite by accident, we found out her bedroom was in one of the alcove rooms near the top of that old mansion. We had been out late one October night prowling around with Funny Norman (more about him later) when we looked down from our hill and saw one light on in the big house. We soon learned that light came from her bedroom window.

With a golden harvest moon gleaming down on us and with the coyotes howling in the hills in that chilly night, we gazed fascinated into that girl's private world and watched her take off all her clothes, one garment at a time. It was a delightful treat for our eyes and the first time my brother and I had ever seen a naked female.

Of course this was all old stuff to Funny Norman who claimed she was just a show-off and knew we were spying on her all the time. Why else would she save her shades up, he said.

My brother and I were too young and shy to have much to do with girls but this "peeping Tom" episode really got us started on the way to biggest and better experiences.

Like the night a few weeks later when we placed a brand new Trojan is the left hand of one of the Forsythe sisters and said, "How about it?" One of the sisters said without hesitation, "Why don't you ask Linda Dodds? She'll be glad to lay for you".

We tried the same thing with other girls later, but sometimes we'd use a wood screw instead of a rubber. These gimmicks never worked. I'd have remembered if they had.

A lot of things happened when we lived in that house and it's strange that I can remember only the little things, like sucking jawbreakers, playing marbles, digging for fishing worms, and not what happened on the big holidays like Christmas or the Fourth of July.

Times slowly got better and dad was lucky enough to get a job as foreman of the new dry pea processing plant. We left the house on the hill and moved to the big house on the north end of town in 1940. Thus started a whole new series of events.

CHAPTER THREE

THE GREAT VIRGIL

Recreation was scarce that bad winter in the early Forties, because the town was snowed in and the basketball tournament had to be canceled.

About all we could do was listen to Jack Armstrong, Captain Midnight. and all those other serials on the radio. One of our favorites was the cowboy movie star hero, Tom Mix, sponsored by the Ralston cereal company. Perhaps because it was so cold it was easy to eat hot cereal every morning but even more than that we wanted to "play square" and be a Ralston Straight Shooter. Also we enjoyed sending for all the decoding rings, badges, etc.

The radio was a great invention because like the telephone. one doesn't have to watch it to enjoy it like with television. Those serials were a godsend because we could chomp on popcorn, l watch the snow coming down, and let our ears and imagination do the rest.

Along with the popcorn and the Ralston hot cereal. we drank lots of Ovaltine and Postum that winter. So did our folks because coffee was rationed.

Sometimes we couldn't even get to school, let alone the movie house, and the war was on so gas was rationed, but we couldn't have driven far anyway because the drifts were so deep.

Even tire chains didn't help much. Especially when parallel parked against the curb between two cars with chunks of ice blocking all four wheels. Rocking back and forth in an attempt to get out might break a chain. All over town we could hear broken chains hanging against fenders as people tried to get around.

Without anti-freeze in the radiators, cars would freeze up and motor blocks would crack. Even when parked in garages, the engines wouldn't start next morning unless a head bolt heater had been plugged in the night before.

Although sugar was rationed also, I do remember eating homemade fudge but because of the shortage of fuel oil, we often had to eat it in bed just to keep warm.

Cigarettes, too, were rationed, and I remember all our parents had those little cigarette-making machines. We'd steal some of their fixings and make out all right but us kids quit smoking anyway after the McCall boys cut loose one Saturday night and accidentally set old man Simm's barn on fire.

Somehow, we never considered smoking and drinking as entertainment. I guess that's because, before the fire, with our corncobs filled with tobacco from stripped butts we picked up. smoking was more a way of life than recreation.

We had our wholesome hobbies, though, and I've always believed in being a doer and not a spectator for the sake of character development, but we could only build model airplanes for so long before eyestrain set in.

I hate to admit it, but out there in the middle of nowhere when it was twenty below on those long evenings, television would have been a blessing.

Today's young people are thrilled by snow because it means skiing and all those other winter sports. Even though winter was a hardship and we were surrounded by vast flat wheat lands unsuitable for skiing, we did have some winter fun. We built snowmen, had snowball wars and ice skated on nearby ponds after we swept the snow off them.

The best part was that we could walk to these activities, without the need for some organized group. There was none of this piling into the back of somebody's father's station wagon for a day's outing. The fathers were always working and we were too young to drive.

Looking back, it was kind of special not to have to depend on public transportation which we had none of anyway or any "manmade" recreation either. We didn't need any help to have fun.

Actually, we were culturally deprived because we didn't have galleries, amusement parks, live theatre productions or any of those refinements that cities offer.

On the plus side, though, we had no racial prejudice. Maybe that's because we didn't have any minority groups. I didn't see a person from another race until I was seventeen years old and never knew what was meant by the term "social problem".

We hadn't much unemployment, little poverty, no labor union problems or strikes, no pollution, no money-grubbing politicians clawing their ways up through government bureaucracies. Were we deprived, missing out on all that?

All us boys had our heroes, however, and because the winters were nine months long, we read a lot of comic books, big-little books, and the Charlie Chan mysteries.

Aside from wanting to be Batman, Robin or Superman, most of us wanted be the usual things like athletes, firemen, or policemen.

Anyway, during that scrotum-tightening winter. I had become fascinated with the adventures of Harry Houdini and had taken up simple card tricks for a diversion. I was too short and small for basketball.

Imagine my excitement then, when I saw this big billboard announcing that a magician was coming to town. He was billed as "The Great Virgil" and the twenty-foot tall picture showed him dressed in black with a mask and a Captain Marvel type cape. The sign said he would prove that the hand is quicker than the eye. It was a thought thrilling enough to make a young kid wet his pants.

Tickets were about five bucks a head, I recall, and I shoveled snow, cut wood, cleaned chicken houses and anything else I could find to scrape up the money.

The program was set for some time in March, to be held in the school auditorium. There was to be one performance only at 8 o'clock at night with no reserved seats.

By the time the date rolled around and the snowplows had opened the roads, I had the dough and was one of the first to buy a ticket.

I wanted to skip school to maybe help the show truck unload but dad wouldn't let me, saying my education was more important than some phony sleight-of-hand artist.

As well as seeing the magic. I wanted tremendously to get The Great Virgil's autograph to go with those jazzy names I'd already collected. Names like Tiger Jack Fox, Chief Spokane, Phil Crosby, Hat Freeman and Rocky Starr.

Wide-eyed. I sat in the front row as I watched the orchestra set up and breathlessly awaited the arrival of the star performer. I was the first one in the gym at about 7 o'clock. Sitting there for a whole hour, I had lots of time to think about magic tricks and Houdini.

I thought about how Houdini could not only saw people in half but escape from chains, safes, handcuffs and water boxes. Some people thought he could dematerialize, but I thought that was a lot of bunk. It was all done with mirrors or something.

The place was packed and as the houselights dimmed, the curtain parted and The Great Virgil stood there in the middle of the stage.

He looked just like the picture on the billboard but with him was this long-legged, blonde girl in red cape, red bra and shorts. A white question mark was on the back of her cape.

I fell in love with that beauty right then but love was nothing new to me, especially after little Nancy in the fifth grade. The second time it was my seventh grade teacher and the third time it was Rocky Starr's vocalist. But this girl was spectacular, especially since she had no ring on her left hand like the others did.

Starling with some simple card tricks which even I could probably do, The Great Virgil moved on up through more and more complicated tricks such as the Chinese Magic Ball Puzzle and one which involved colored scarves in a mailing tube.

His lovely assistant he introduced as Ginny, and mostly she just danced around handing him things and moving props. She helped him through the Bavarian Hoop Trick and had us all squealing when she got in a long box and The Great Virgil made like he sawed her in half.

Then The Great Virgil asked for a young man from the audience to assist him and all us kids were waving our arms and yelling like crazy to be picked. The kid selected sat right next to me, a dumb runt named Dickie Slocum who didn't know enough about magic to put on the head of a pin. I tried to trip him as he got up but he lifted his foot just in time.

The trick was as old as the hills. The old collapsing wand trick. The Great Virgil kept handing it to Dickie and it kept going limp as everyone laughed.

Then came Madame Guillotine. The stage hands and Ginny wheeled out this guillotine contraption about twenty feet tall and The Great Virgil asked Dickie what it was.

Dickie didn't know so it was explained to him and the audience that it was stolen from France where they used it to cut off people's heads. Some red stuff had been smeared on the blade to try to fool everybody into thinking it was real blood.

The magician then demonstrated its use by cutting a few cabbages in two and eating the pieces, trying to get Dickie to eat some, too. Then he told Dickie if he was really brave and had his life insurance paid up he could help in the demonstration. About then, Dickie started running off the stage, especially when he was told accidents sometimes happen.

Five big bruisers finally got Dickie back on the stage and shoved his head on the block while his mother fidgeted in the back row.

Down came the blade and Dickie screamed but kept his head. I wish it could have been me up there. It might be old hat but that trick was still exciting.

As Dickie was leaving the stage, The Great Virgil reached down the back of Dickie's shirt and pulled out a big old Canadian goose and accused Dickie of trying to steal his property.

Dickie looked guilty as hell as The Great Virgil then reached down the front of Dickie's pants and pulled out about a million different items including a hamster, colored handkerchiefs, a white rat and a couple of turtledoves — everything but a rabbit. We all about died laughing.

It was about 10:30 by that time and the show was heading for the finale as the tricks got more and more exciting with the magician throwing knives at Ginny and shooting ribbons through her and getting out of handcuffs while blindfolded and all stuff like that.

The final trick was one in which the mighty prestidigitator was going to attempt to escape from a big wooden box. I had seen the box before because the Senior Class boys had built it in woodshop class especially for this show.

About a dozen people were called out of the audience to inspect the thing and make sure that the nails were real and the box was actually the same one the class had made for this trick.

The stage was thoroughly inspected to see there were no trap doors or mirrors or anything.

Then the magician sent everyone back to their seats and called for another young assistant. I was passed over again in favor of this older guy named Elmer Peters, I think his name was, and he was a clownish oaf that was probably retarded. Today, he'd be put in a special school.

Anyway, Elmer went up on stage grinning like a lovesick idiot at Ginny and The Great Virgil produced a big canvas bag which he asked Elmer to inspect to see there were no holes in it. Meanwhile, Ginny was sitting in the box to show how a person would look inside it.

All of a sudden Elmer ran across the stage and jumped in the box with Ginny and the crowd roared. I was too naive to even suspect Elmer could have been a well-rehearsed plant.

I'll never forget what happened next. It stands out in my memory as clearly as if it was yesterday, Instead of about thirty-five years ago.

The Great Virgil walked to the center of the stage and as the lights dimmed and a blue spotlight hit him, he said. "Watch closely, ladies and gentlemen, for the more you watch. the less you see!"

Then they got Elmer out and the magician was blindfolded and handcuffed and about a hundred feet of chain were wrapped around him and padlocked.

The Great Virgil was placed inside the bag inside the box and the bag was tied with thick rope. Then the boys from the shop class came up and Ginny handed them hammers and nails and they fastened the lid down and left the stage.

Some more people were called up to look around and talk to the magician to prove that he was still in the box and there were no mirrors or funny stuff happening.

Ginny then put a transparent veil of cheesecloth over the box and the audience had to sit quietly for five minutes listening to some eerie music.

Ginny then called two of the shop boys up again and they ripped open the box. The bag was empty and The Great Virgil was gone. We never saw him again. The box was dumped over and all that chain, rope and stuff poured out. With great stage presence, Ginny bowed. showing her legs and a lot of cleavage, and the curtain closed.

I sat there and waited until everyone went home and finally crept backstage, thinking The Great Virgil was hiding someplace. Mr. Morrison. the janitor, was sweeping up and I asked him If he had seen anyone sneaking around under the stage or in the wings. He told me. "No, I ain't seen no. body". so I went out back and the show truck was gone.

I went home and thought about what I'd seen for a long time after that. Mostly. I thought about what I didn't see. Especially the way The Great Virgil escaped. I sure did want his autograph.

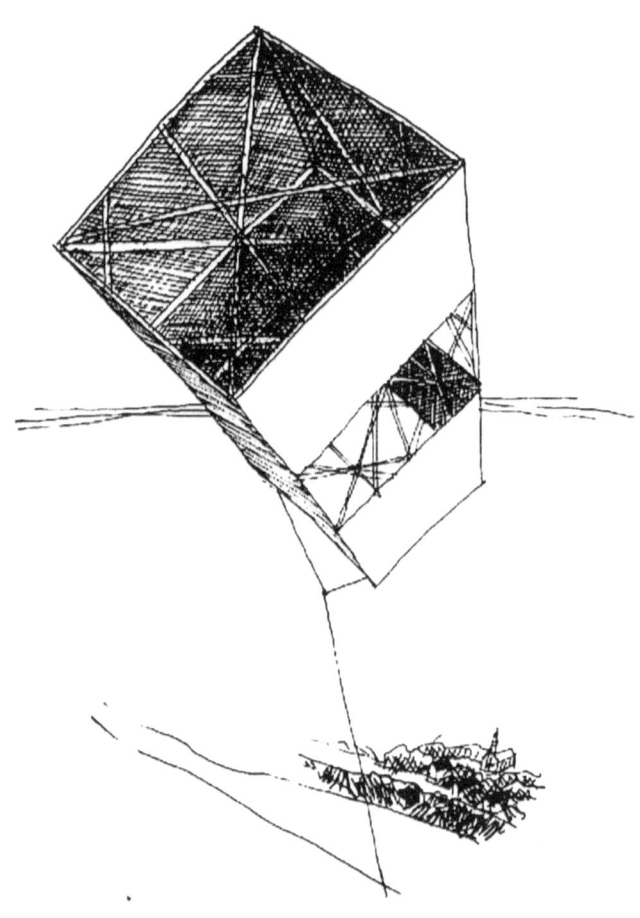

CHAPTER FOUR

THE MAIDEN FLIGHT OF THE WINDSOCKET

So it was in that dusty little wheat town south of Spokane. I spent my boyhood during the late 1930's. But this tale is about a guy named Morris Weintraub. In 1939 he was a senior in high school, and I was just a hero worshipping third grader.

Morris was the Huckleberry Finn type that was never meant for the rigors of formal education. He was the kind of undisciplined savage that would have thrived had he been born during the early days when the West was really wild.

A constant troublemaker, he climbed out the window of a third-floor classroom one afternoon and walked completely around the building on a six-inch ledge with all those teachers and students gawking and yelling at him. No, Morris was never meant for the three R's. A lot of kids today were never meant for them either.

Just a few years ago, that would have been considered a radical, Un-American statement but recently we've seen an upsurge in the popularity of the vocational college, commonly referred to as the "trade school". Morris was prime trade school material because he was a natural craftsman. What he lacked in the academics he made up for in practical skills.

An enterprising individual, Morris had two paper routes and delivered papers on the town's only motor bike, one he built himself from spare parts Old Man Ryan junked in his backyard garage.

He was a talented cartoonist and sold his cartoons to the local weekly paper. Later, he became the unsung originator of the first pornographic cartoon.

To ward off lethargy, he worked after school and Saturdays at the butcher shop. With charisma alone, he could sell green hamburger to housewives and became famous for his two-pound thumb. Today, he'd be called a con artist.

His artistic bent carried him into the world of music and I remember more than once going to the auditorium on a Saturday night to hear one of his recitals. Usually it was the accordion but he could also play the violin and piano with equal dexterity.

Later, he put a bunch of horns, drums and other paraphernalia together and billed himself as "Morris, the One-Man Band". He transported all this stuff in an old Dodge truck and played at country dances in Grange halls on Saturday nights.

He could play a saw, a washboard, and a bass viol. He could blow a jug or play the ocarina, trumpet, Jew's harp or flute. Small wonder he had no time for the academics.

And yet I never really knew him even if he was a legend in his own time. Most of this information about him was handed down to me from older boys.

But aviation was his greatest challenge. He started by building gigantic balsa-wood gliders in the school's wood shop.

Our school building was one of those big square three-storied atrocities popular in that era that housed the high schoolers on the top floor, the grade school kids on the second, and the wood shop, home ec rooms, gym, and boiler room were on the street level.

Looking back, it seems incredible that over two-hundred kids were enrolled in that ancient gray relic which looked for all the world like a medieval castle.

Now the shop was supposed to be off limits to us in the lower grades but sometimes we'd sneak down to have a peek. There we'd see Morris laboring away. He spent so much time in that shop that those of us in the third grade thought he was the teacher at first. In his long white coat, he did look like an instructor and even the shop teacher would ask for his advice on projects.

Morris's gliders got bigger and bigger until he eventually built the granddaddy of them all, the huge seven-foot wing span "Condor" model and flew it over the school yard one noon hour. That glider flew straight up, heading for the sun but something went wrong. Maybe a bird or a falling star hit it but anyway it came just as straight down and smashed into a hundred pieces.

Setbacks like that never bothered Morris. One lunch period, after, he'd graduated from gliders to gasoline-powered aircraft, an expensive biplane of his broke its line and hit a stop sign, splitting the plane in two. He philosophically picked up the pieces and went back to his worktable.

Morris had that kind of faith that made Daedalus take wax and glue them together so he and his son, Icarus, could escape from that island prison. It is that kind of faith that was characteristic of Leonardo da Vinci, the Wright Brothers, and Charles Lindberg.

Now. let me again discuss education and the manual arts. That shop teacher was a skilled craftsman but a lousy instructor. He had been teaching shop courses most of his life but he didn't teach Morris anything and years later, he didn't teach me anything either.

During just one year of my manual training requirements, that instructor built himself a boat, a dining room set, and a roll-top desk. Few students completed anything.

I started out in September to make a mahogany cedar chest for my mother. I glued the boards for the sides together but I could never seem to get them smooth enough to pass the instructor's standards. Instead of helping me, he just kept me sanding and planning those boards until nothing was left but sawdust. That was expensive sawdust but cheap training!

A classmate of mine planned to make a black walnut china closet for his mother but couldn't get any help on the mortise and tenon joints so gave up and decided to convert his masterpiece into a rabbit hutch. It would have been the most expensive rabbit hutch in the world but he never finished it and the rabbits died.

Anyway, the *Windsocket* was Morris's greatest triumph. At first we didn't even know what it was. We knew it wasn't a plane or a glider because of all its square corners but for months we saw it taking shape in the hallway. That was strange to us also because we thought all projects were supposed to be kept locked inside the shop. Then we realized that no high school shop in the United States would have been big enough to accommodate the *world's largest box kite*!

Built in four sections, it was twenty feet long and ten feet wide, made of wire, fish line, muslin bed sheets, and balsa slats. We skipped recesses and lunch just to watch Morris work on it.

He carefully drilled holes, cut notches, glued in the struts and supports, fastened little metal braces in the corners and then stretched the sheets over the framework. Then he got out a lot of strong-smelling lacquers and shellacs and sprayed everything. When they dried, the sheets were tight every part of the kite was rigid, hard, and coated smooth.

Finally, on the Friday before St. Patrick's Day, he finished the Windsocket. Morris had hoped to take the kite out through the gym past the boiler room but on that day the boiler overheated and the janitor was afraid the school might blow up so everyone was evacuated. School was dismissed for the day.

Anyway, that route would have meant taking out a lot of doors, walls, and window frames, plus moving loads of bleachers and athletic equipment.

Therefore, we had no choice but to inch it along the lower hall to the school's front entrance. There we were stopped; it wouldn't go through the doors. Morris got permission to remove the large double doors, and with about ten kids and the instructor all helping, the Windsocket breathed fresh air at last.

We helped Morris load the kite into a rickety trailer hitched to his old Dodge and he started off through town with the shopkeepers and townspeople all gaping at the earthbound monster. They just stopped what they were doing and lined the main drag with their hands on their hips, scratching their heads and clucking in wonderment. We all followed on our bikes.

The road wound up a gravel road, around hairpin turns for five miles until we reached the top of one of the two hills that bordered the valley. Below was the town. The winds were steady and strong but not gusting. Perfect kite-flying weather!

With us was this kid we called Johnny Reb because he was a devilish rebel, a perfect pint-sized protégé version of Morris. Morris used his slide rule to calculate weight and decided that Johnny, the smallest kid in school had two pounds to spare and would fly the Windsocket on its maiden flight.

Morris had rigged up a little seat, and Johnny was put aboard, much to the envy of every one of us.

With a special reel attached to his chest, Morris made ready. The reel was filled with expensive nylon cord, a hard-to-get item in those days even though the war hadn't yet started.

I was one of the honored three that got to hold one of the lines Morris had tied to his waist to prevent being pulled into the air along with the Windsocket.

The kite lifted off. We held onto Morris. The wind tipped the Windsocket at a crazy angle, and I thought Johnny would be dumped out. Then it righted itself. Soon the kite with its human cargo soared at least a thousand feet above our town. All of us yelled and jumped up and down like crazy with excitement.

The winds blew harder. The kite soared higher, and Morris fought both wind and rope to keep his feet. We had to fight to hold Morris. Once he was lifted up into the air. We had a hard time holding him and it's a wonder we didn't pull his pants off, but Butch Hollister, Chuck Smollet and I all had death grips on those lines and the wide leather belt Morris was wearing.

Bill Biggers had snitched his old man's binoculars and I got a hasty glimpse of Johnny's face. He was laughing and yelling. The rest of us begged Morris to haul in Johnny and give us a ride.

About then, a white-faced woman burst through the throng. She was crying and screaming, hysterically pulling her hair. Bill Biggers told us she was Johnny's mother but we couldn't understand why she was so upset.

Johnny's old lady just kept on screaming, beating on Morris's back and pointing at Windsocket which by then was a tiny dot in front of the sun.

Morris remained unflustered. He was calm and cool. That's what I really remember as I think back on that afternoon, the godlike amazing coolness and self-confidence of that nonconforming individualist!

"Oh, my God, please bring him down. He'll be killed, you horrid boy!" the woman kept screaming and calling Morris all kinds of bad names.

All too soon Morris started slowly reeling in Windsocket and Johnny. We all helped ease the kite gently to the ground. Morris lit a cigarette while Johnny's mother, still blubbering, snatched her kid out of the seat.

We all watched, wide-eyed, as she kissed and hugged that embarrassed little kid; as though Johnny had been in some danger the way she carried on.

Anyway, Morris graduated in May. I remember it well because it was such an unseasonably hot night and I had to wear my one good pair of itchy wool tweed pants.

I saw Morris once or twice after that, delivering his papers or tinkering with his planes but I lost all trace of Windsocket. I never saw Morris fly it again and I wonder if it was because Johnny's parents had threatened to sue him.

They never did sue him, however, and lawsuits were rare then. Especially when they had to do with "emotional stress' and fancy words like "duress" and "grievous mental agony". And all because Johnny's mother had a nervous breakdown over nothing.

In 1943, when I was twelve, Morris drifted out of town to some job in a neighboring town. Then I heard he became a mechanic for Boeings in Seattle. Later, I found out he had joined the Army Air Force.

Still later, after I had taken over those paper routes, I happened to glance at a back page of one of the big dailies I was delivering and read that Morris had been killed when his plane went down somewhere in the Pacific.

I'll always wonder if he, like Icarus, flew too close to the sun and the glue melted from his feathers.

CHAPTER FIVE

HORSE TALES

Some people rave about how intelligent and noble horses are. My experience has been that the beasts are stubborn, stupid and unpredictable. Besides that, they smell bad.

I wouldn't know an Arabian from an Appaloosa nor a quarter horse from a walker, but I do know they all burn hay and the expense of their upkeep makes them a bad investment and a damn nuisance for the average person. They are obsolete and will never replace dogs and cats as domestic pets.

Also, except for the rock-hard guts of cowboy movie stars, the average normal male's anatomy was not designed for horseback riding.

However, women and horses seem to belong together. Maybe that's why television commercials show pictures of young girls galloping horses along beaches or across deserts. To see those beauties with their hair and the horses' manes flowing in the wind is indeed a spectacle and undoubtedly sells lots of shampoo.

My dislike for horses goes way back to the first time I ever rode a horse in the early spring of 1947 when I was sixteen years old.

My little brother's a part of the story too. He and I were town kids but we had a couple of friends that lived on farms and the four of us decided on this big spring camping trip with pack horses and all.

Kids today get experience around horses from riding ponies in amusement parks and riding stables but we didn't have those things in my hometown. Not even a merry-go-round.

So anyway, two weeks before the camping trip which was making my brother and I so excited, something else happened which we should have seen as an omen but we were too stupid.

We had this character on a ranch out in the hills known as Old Widow Sally. She'd come to town wearing a lavender print skirt over her bib overalls and had made herself leggings out of gunny sacks which reached up out of sight under the skirt. White hair stuck out under a black Stetson which almost hid her lean and hard features. I never saw her smile. She was old then and so tough she's probably still alive and that was over thirty years ago.

My father was night marshall then, and part-time bartender in the only tavern and sometimes I was in the bar when Old Widow Sally would come in. She reminded me of an old Indian squaw with her tan face, sitting at the bar and chewing tobacco just like a man.

She was even built like a man, no curves or anything. Probably lots of people never knew she was a woman; except the other women in town. They knew! And they thought she was a disgrace to their sex!

Even though it was in the early Forties and most everybody had cars, Old Widow Sally came to town in a wagon pulled by a team of chestnut work horses. It was rumored she was filthy rich but didn't want a car and never even learned to drive one.

Dad used to talk about her and I think he even talked to her but I never heard her say anything because she sort of mumbled.

Us kids were all scared of her because she seemed like such an eccentric old character and never laughed, just looked grim and mean. Of course she really wasn't. She was just tired, hard-working and practical, a liberated female doing her thing.

Well, dad was behind the bar one afternoon and I happened to be there playing with the cigar lighter when somebody comes running in yelling "Old Widow Sally's in trouble!"

It seems she's on her way to Spokane which is over thirty-six miles away and has had an accident with the team and wagon.

Dad and I pile in our old 36 Chevvy and head out. We find the old gal over twenty miles from town. She's in a ditch and the wagon is tipped over with harness and reins and sacks of wheat, peas and produce scattered all over the highway.

What happened is some smart-aleck driver forced her off the road and boy, is she mad! Dad's embarrassed that I have to hear her language because she's sitting there in that mess swearing like a drunken sailor and shaking her fist at the drivers and screaming at the sky like an Indian doing a war dance.

Dad gets her calmed down and he and I and some other drivers get her wagon turned back upright and the horses untangled while she's got this long whip jut beating the devil out of those plugs.

Old Widow Sally climbs back up on the seat and moves on as if nothing had happened. Today, she'd have been given a citation for having horses on a highway but dad just told her to be careful and stay over on the shoulder as far as she can.

The driver that caused the accident is gone as usual in such cases so dad and I go back to the bar. I see right then one drawback to horses. They don't fit in a mechanized world and seem to have outlived their usefulness. Yet more people own horses for pleasure or profit today than ever before and more horses are around now than during the time of the Indians.

But back to that camping trip! I remember how the four of us laughed with fiendish glee as we made ready because we planned to skip a couple of days' school to get an early start. This was because of the Teacher's Institute which fell in April that year between Easter vacation and the end of school in early June.

The Institute was to start on a Monday and school was to be closed for a week but the four of us bugged out on a noon of the previous Wednesday.

My brother and I had all the wrong gear and clothes and only cheap army surplus sleeping bags and no knapsacks. We just threw some pants and shirts and cooking pans into two old pillow cases of our mother's.

I remember how embarrassed I was because my pillowcase had two hearts sewn on it with a cupid's dart through them.

Years later my parents divorced but it wasn't until recently that I thought back on those symbolic hearts and the irony of it all.

Marve and Dave were the two country kids and the plan was to drive the two-hundred or so miles into the Okanogan Highlands, to Marve's dad's cattle ranch near the Canadian border and then pack into the mountains it from there.

We threw everything into the back of Marve's pickup and by the time we reached the ferry, crossed Lake Roosevelt above Grand Coulee Dam and reached the ranch house, it was still light enough to see patches of snow in the pastures and rain was pouring down.

None of us expected this kind of weather in April so we were unprepared except possibly Marve who always seemed to have all the right stuff for any kind of conditions.

It was too late to do much the first night so Marve's dad sat us down for a social evening and introduced us all around. There was Cliff, the ranch foreman and his young pregnant wife who looked like she swallowed a watermelon. How white and out of place that woman looked in that rugged mountain country!

There was also Josie, a hired girl who mostly just giggled and made big eyes at us as she helped around the kitchen.

Then there was Charley and Bill, the two hands. Both were lean and rawboned. Bill walked with a limp and Marve said he used to be a rodeo rider and had all of his bones broken at least once. Everybody seemed to belong in this setting except my brother and I and Cliffs wife and I knew even then that that country could be hard on a woman!

We had supper and sat around awhile, my brother and I staring wide-eyed at the mounted deer heads on the walls and even the gun racks were made from antlers and hooves of game. The homemade furniture was surrounded by rustic knotty-pine walls.

They gave my brother and I a back bedroom and when we have just finished our nightly joke-telling and wrestling, we climbed in on a straw tick mattress under a patchwork quilt blanket. It was the first time either of us had ever slept on a setup like that.

Just as we were getting settled down after throwing each other out of bed at least once, we hear a knock on the door and in comes Cliff's young pregnant wife.

Well, she came real close and bent over to tuck us in. Boy, did she ever smell good! I thought I was a little old to be tucked in but I didn't say anything and then she kissed us both on our foreheads. With her warm breath and that woman smell it was really stimulating. She carried a flickering kerosene lamp and in the shadows I couldn't see none too good but I could have found that woman without half trying even if it was totally dark!

About 3:30 a.m., she started having labor pains and we could hear all hell breaking loose downstairs with her screaming and all so Cliff loaded her into a pickup and drove her the twenty miles over bad roads into a hospital at Tonasket.

That ruined the night for sleeping so we stayed up while Josie fixed us the biggest breakfast I ever had. I thought the supper was big but that girl brought out mountains of bacon and eggs, ham and toast, pancakes, hash brown potatoes, hot cereal, all of which we washed down with plenty of orange juice and coffee.

I was soon to find out why the meals were so big. This was a working ranch and they meant to put us to work.

While it was still dark, they put all four of us boys in the back of a hay wagon and we headed for the pastures where we sweated with those pitchforks tossing hay out to beef cattle as we drove between the snow patches.

When that was done, we pitched more hay out of the barn into the wagon for the evening's feeding.

The cows were all dropping their calves at that time of the year and we got word that one of those range cows was having trouble birthing her calf somewhere on the south ridge.

Marve's dad had already left so Bill got us a couple of horses to ride out there. Boy, did Charley laugh when I got on that horse in the rain in that plastic raincoat with buttons all down the front. He stood there and said "Don't mind me, I just want to see a man mount a horse with a raincoat on!"

Well, I did everything wrong including getting up on the right side and of course those coat buttons popped off in all directions while everybody laughed.

It was decided my brother would ride with Dave and I was on old Prince behind Marve so that meant four boys on two horses but maybe it was a good idea because I didn't even know where the starter was.

After about a mile I was aching in every joint. The walk and the gallop weren't bad but that rough trot really shook up my breakfast and rubbed my thighs raw. Of course none of this bothered Marve because he was used to it and had on those thick leather chaps with his name on them.

When we finally got there, Marve's dad had his right arm clear up to the armpit inside that cow. It seems the calf was stillborn and Marve's dad was trying to turn the calf to get it out in one piece. He had a hook on a nylon rope and was trying to wrap it around something. Seems like he said he was able to get an eyesocket but I don't remember exactly. Anyway, he had Charley and Bill and the four of us boys all pull on that rope like we were having, a tug of war and finally we see the tiny front legs coming out. Marve's dad tucks them back in and soon we see this ugly little head appear. We all heave as hard as we can be making blisters on our hands and out comes that blue colored calf with a lot of gooey afterbirth.

What was really amazing was after a few minutes the cow gets up, relieves herself of some more afterbirth and staggers off. That cow knew her calf was dead before it was born because she sniffed it once and never looked back.

After that, we all just sort of wipe off our hands in the snow after burying the calf and someone pulls some lunch stuff out of one of the saddlebags and we gulp that down real fast and mount up again.

We soon find ourselves riding fence down on the lower ranges and handing tools to Bill and Charley. It's about three o'clock by then and I can see that these guys never take any rest breaks because they never get tired! They just keep going from dawn to dark. They don't make men like that nowadays!

All of those guys from Marlboro country would look like sissies compared to these ranch hands. Cliff was probably the most domesticated because he was married and smoked Camels but Bill and Charley scoffed at tailor-made cigarettes. Either of them could roll a cigarette with one hand while sitting a horse in a windstorm.

Purple shadows were stretched across the hills when we finished the fence work and headed back. We slept in the pastures that night and next day, the men engaged in some fancy riding and roping and earmarked a few calves and castrated a string of horses.

All this seemed kind of bloody and brutal to a couple of city kids, especially seeing Bill cut those horses and nonchalantly whistle as he wiped the blood off his jackknife on his chaps and stick it back in his pocket.

Of course my brother and I didn't know the difference between a gelding, a stud or a stallion and still don't but it was kind of interesting anyway.

We pulled up to a range corral just before dark and inside I saw three gigantic Brahma bulls. The men explain the bulls are too heavy to rope and throw so they earmark them standing and brand them with some dye which they paint on with brushes. Just as if they were using branding irons, those brands smoke and smell like burning flesh and the bulls buck and rear. Boy, it was all like a wild west show but I'm so dog-tired by then I can't enjoy it.

Well, we get back to the ranch house and the smoke is curling out of the chimney and it sure looks warm and cozy. I'm glad to be back. like coming out of a war or something and Josie runs out to meet us all flirty and coy. She fixes us another of those monstrous meals and we turn in early cause we plan to pack into the mountains in the morning.

Josie tells us that Cliffs wife hasn't had the baby yet and it was false labor but figuring on the unsettled weather and all they decide she should stay in the hospital anyway. Cliff leaves again right after supper to stay with her until the kid is born.

Next morning Marve, Dave, and my brother and I roll out of bed real early again. Only this time we eat breakfast and start to get our things together, telling everybody with a laugh not to work too hard while we're on vacation and kind of rubbing it in Charlie and Bill cause we're going camping and they're not.

We bring Prince and an old mare around front and start putting the duffle aboard em and all the time I'm being real careful that nobody can see that pillowcase with the two hearts on it and all that other worthless gear I'm carrying like my old Kodak, a diary and some writing paper. We tie the sleeping bags up behind the saddles, the rifles in the scabbards and gallop off, four boys on two horses again while everybody laughs again.

We're hardly out of sight behind the house when the going gets about straight up and soon we notice the snow is getting deeper. The horses are floundering up to their flanks in the stuff and lunging and rearing so much we finally take the hint and get off and lead 'em awhile. Then we're all floundering around up to our hips in snow.

All day we keep climbing and just as the horses and us are about exhausted, we reach this old line cabin that Marve knows about. We settle in there for the night and after chasing the rats off the tables, we clean off four old crude bunks and roll out our sleeping bags. We feed the horses some grain and sack out.

Early next morning Marve sets to work with his oversized hands and soon the talented little devil is making candleholders, plates and silverware out of old tin cans, rebuilding furniture, making repairs of all kinds and the place starts to look like a home.

We decided to lay over for a day since the cabin has become so comfortable and spend the time exploring and out target shooting with the rifle and a .22 caliber pistol we brought along.

We spot a hill that's loaded with rabbits so we take turns pretending we're old-time gunfighters and take pot shots at those bunnies. It's a wonder we didn't kill each other trying our quick draws and shooting up the landscape. The rabbits had nothing to worry about.

I forgot to mention that Marve was a "testicle-grabber". Mostly, he was just a playful clown that loved to wrestle. He was younger and smaller than any of us but that didn't stop him from wrestling us down under the legs of the horses and engaging us in snowball fights that lasted for an hour.

The following day we load up again and hike all day leading the horses ever higher through snow to another line shack where we make camp again.

By now we're in the Chelan National Forest and start the climb up Tunk Mountain to a lookout tower. On the way we cross the Canadian border. I don't know what we're expecting but it's sort of a letdown because we see no markers or anything. Just a swath cut through the timber on the high ridges stretching away out of sight.

We climb toward the lookout and in the late afternoon I'm on the back of Prince behind Marve when Prince steps on a branch which makes a loud snap and it really startles the old boy because he swerves his hind end around a couple of times. I feel myself flying through the air, over the sleeping bags and rolling head over heels back down the side of Tunk Mountain. I land in a pine tree, shook up and scared but unhurt.

Mostly, I'm mad and just plain fed up with horseflesh and having to depend on something as unpredictable as a dumb animal.

Now horses are just like any other animals and if God had intended for men to ride them, horses would be born with men on their backs. For some men, the horse is an extension of themselves, just like a gun or a high-powered automobile and it makes them feel superior and self-confident. Some experts insist all this has something to do with Freud and the male sex organ but how would I know?

The Spaniards broke the horse to ride and marched into Mexico conquering the Indians while smugly looking down from atop their steeds. Later, the American Indian undoubtedly felt some of that same smugness when he too conquered the horse. I still maintain, along with a lot of veterinarians that a horse's back was not designed for a human being to straddle.

I guess all this is why still today I like to see movies of those wild bands of riderless Mustangs racing free across the prairies.

Anyway, we make it back to the line shack and spend the night there. Sometime the night before, Marve must have cut his hand on something and it got infected.

He never mentioned the cut to any of us but soon we noticed the black streak moving up his forearm. We didn't know anything about blood poisoning but I had read someplace that by the time the black streak had moved up the arm and out to the heart, the person's croaked.

Of course this was all poppycock but I told the others we better not wait around to see whether I was right or wrong. We headed back, pushing hard and make it back to the ranch after about driving the horses to death.

We pull onto the home range and up to the ranch house expecting a hero's welcome. I guess, so we're really disappointed when nobody comes out to meet us. Bill and Charley are doing some carpentry work down behind the bunkhouse and we can hear the hammering but they don't hardly even look up when we ride by.

Marve's dad comes out and loads Marve into a pickup for the trip into the Tonasket hospital and Josie starts flitting around like some drunken butterfly but nobody gets too excited.

My brother and I go inside and there's Cliff's wife, sitting in a maple rocker with her blouse undone nursing a baby. She smiles when she sees us and that warm smile is like beautiful sunshine engulfing the room.

Her happiness hits us like a ton of bricks as we're standing there all tired and dirty gaping at her naked breasts and soft, pale face. I think of the unhappy face on that cow with the dead calf and I remember somebody telling me sometime that the Lord giveth and the Lord taketh away. I might have read it somewhere but it was probably my mother or some Sunday school teacher who told it to me a long time ago.

Of course I'm so happy to be back safe and alive my emotions are raising bell inside me and seeing that woman and child like they're the Virgin Mary and Jesus I feel like I'm going to bust out crying.

Well, Cliff's wife insists we hold the baby even if we are dirty as if she feels it'll do something for us and she's right! I hold that kid in my arms and I'm suddenly warm all over, especially my insides.

Next morning we leave and I think a lot about what happened for a long time later. It occurs to me now I never even knew what Cliffs wife's first name was. Or her last name either.

That's about all I have to say about horses except that I would never want to own one. Also, if I'd have known this essay would have been so long and include a character description, one short story, and a lot of digression. I never would have written it.

CHAPTER SIX

THE GENTLE ART

Winter can come early in eastern Washington so after that last frosty night football game in 1946, we prep school athletes retreated to the cozier climate of the gymnasium.

It was a boring, in-between period for us but it gave the coach a little time to prepare for basketball season.

Some of us were too short for basketball and the chilly days with their heavy rains kept the playing fields and tracks too sloppy for any outdoor sport.

About then, somebody came up with the idea of Tumbleball one noon hour while the rest of us were engaged in a combination marble and ping-pong tournament which raged in the upper hallways. Trying to play marbles on slicked varnished floors leaves much to be desired and it gets dull waiting one's turn to play on only one scratched ping-pong table. Maybe that's partly why we considered something new.

For the unfamiliar, Tumbleball is played with a gigantic balloon-type ball and totally without rules. The object of the game is to grab the ball and run with it until the ball is taken away by another player or the ball carrier is knocked unconscious, whichever occurs first.

On the ball someone had written in blood. "KILL OR BE KILLED". I didn't know what that meant until we started the game and I accidently caught the ball in my skinny arms and started to run with it.

What happened next reminded me of the night a month earlier when Funny Norman (more about him later) caught a fumble during the opening kick-off of a football game and was upended with twenty players on top of him; half ours and half theirs. Both of us should have known better. Now, years later, the wounds have healed and I can begin to see some humor in it.

Disliking the violent nature of Tumbleball, I decided to embark on a career in pugilism, the sport of gentlemen. Also, since I would never marry. I knew my life would be fraught with adventure and danger at every turn so I had best learn how to defend myself.

Mostly I saw myself as a crime fighter, a guardian of the weak and oppressed, a champion of justice, and defender of the truth. The gentle art of boxing somehow appealed to me aesthetically and hopefully would satisfy the more sensitive sides of my inner nature.

Now, I've always had prejudices against team sports because I never liked the idea of having to depend on one's teammates to win. It seemed far nobler in my mind to stand alone against an opponent, far more courageous to win by myself. I confess I thought only about the fruits of victory and never about the agony of defeat.

The first requirement was to go buy an athletic supporter, commonly referred to as a "jock strap". The coach said that in the actual bouts we'd use steel-plated ones which are regulation boxing gear but that the regular kind would be okay for normal use.

I already had a jock strap which I had used for football season and I didn't want to buy another because of the embarrassing experience I'd had getting the first one.

Jock straps can be purchased in any sporting goods store or even most hardware stores anywhere in the world. But our town didn't have a sporting goods store and the hardware man said he didn't know what I was talking about when I requested an "athletic supporter".

Anyway, we did have a drugstore but when I went up to the counter that fall a female clerk who was an older friend of my sisters' stood ready to wait on me. She kept asking, "What is it you're looking for, Bobby?"

I was plenty flustered and stalled around until the pharmacist finished making up a prescription and turned to see what I wanted. I'm humiliated to confess that druggist was such a super salesman he sent me from this store not with an athletic supporter but with one of those hernia trusses that old men who have been ruptured use. This was just another example of how small our town was.

Well, I had to make another trip to Spokane to get the real McCoy even if I thought I could make it through the boxing season without a spare jock strap and everything worked out okay even if I did double park in front of the Spokesman-Review building and get dad's car towed away and impounded.

The conditioning began with hours spent in the sweat box, miles of road work, sparring practice, and many kinds of bending exercises.

I don't know what made me think I had the aggressive nature of a killer but it was easy to beat the devil out of the punching bag or that big canvass sack we used which didn't hit back.

Just before I'd decided to be a boxer I had taken a job working in the butcher shop nights after school and my back and shoulders were in pretty good shape from scraping the butcher's block, sweeping the floor, and tonging big blocks of ice around.

The butcher fancied himself a comedian, nicknamed me "Tiger" and would try to position me with his friends when they came in, all just in fun. Usually about then, he had to throw down his apron and catch the fire truck going by since he was a member of the volunteers'.

The butcher's helper, a kid so fat he was almost round, almost knocked me through the front window one night while we were demonstrating how hard my stomach muscles were. After that I'd just lie on the floor and let the kid jump on me awhile. What nobody knew was that I was sneaking into the freezer and using those sides of beef for punching bags but a lot of that meat was destined to become just hamburger anyway.

As I recall, there were only a half dozen of us on the boxing team. The other guys turned out for basketball, that is, all but the pool sharks and the athletically hopeless.

This latter group was used by us sometimes as sparring partners. Of course, we used no helmets or mouthpieces during sparring sessions and just had at each other. One of these guys and I stood toe to toe and slugged it out til we were both bloody. Neither of us was smart enough to duck. Another kid, a gangly farm boy wearing clodhoppers was so screwy looking that while watching his antics I got clobbered by a haymaker he brought up from the floor. It was the only time I'd been knocked down.

In early January, the coach declared us ready and set up matches for us in neighboring town.

I was then 123 pounds of rock-hard fighting fury in excellent shape. The only guy on the team smaller than I was a shrimp who had polio as a kid. He was to fight in the 115 pound bracket. In our boxing trunks we must have looked like a couple of bobby pins wearing band aids.

On the windy night of January 15, 1947, we boarded the coach's station wagon and travelled 25 miles to a small town near the border between Idaho and Washington.

Mine was to be the second bout on the card and I sat with a cold ball of fear in my guts as I watched my 116 pound teammate fight to a draw after three five minute rounds.

All too soon I was in the ring on my tiny stool beside the coach. Hands and wrist taped, he pulled the 16 pound gloves over my fingers and jammed the rubber mouthpiece between my jaws.

Icy talons of dread were creeping up from my stomach into my throat as the coach reached outside the ring and grabbed a large jar of Vaseline. He started rubbing the stuff all over me with his cold fingers and telling me that when I started tasting Vaseline I was getting hit too often so I should fight harder.

The theory was that the Vaseline would make my opponent's blows slip off me and not leave bruises. Some consolation!

I looked out into the darkness where the spectators sat and could see the glowing ends of their cigarettes. I smelled the penetrating odors of tobacco, popcorn, coffee, sweat, liniment, and that blasted Vaseline.

Looking up, I saw insects circling in the smoke drifting around the huge ring light and in the dim outlines of the shadowy balconies where sat other spectators eager for blood and gore.

Then I looked across the ring at my opponent who was a tall. thin, black headed kid. I hadn't wanted to look at him until absolutely necessary. How ugly he looked when his coach put his mouthpiece in place and he stood up pulling the ring ropes and rubbing his shoes in the rosin box.

I saw the crowd as my enemy. This wasn't my home town. They wouldn't want me to win and I knew I'd be on my own out there.

The referee beckoned to both of us and as we met in the center of the ring to receive instructions I noticed how much taller than me my opponent was.

The referee said, "Let's have a clean fight. I want you to break when I tell you to. Watch the low blows. If your opponent is knocked down, go to a neutral corner and wait until I tell you to come out. Any questions? Now go to your corners. Good luck and may the best man win!"

The bell rang and we both ran out and touched gloves. It was then I felt such fear as I've never known before and forgot everything I knew about boxing. If I ever knew anything about it at all. Was it feint with the right or the left? Was it bob and weave or weave and bob?

Wanting to be offensive from the beginning and sickened by the thought of possibly being knocked unconscious, I wind milled my way through my adversary's long arms.

I knew if I could once get inside, I'd have him but he kept dodging and weaving as I kept charging and wind milling. Soon he was running backwards, jabbing with his left and I couldn't seem to tag him. Why hadn't I taken time to feel him out and savvy his style? I guess it was because I was too scared to do anything but make it a slugfest.

The crowd loved it and were on their feet, snarling like a pack of mad dogs. I knew even then that man is basically a violent animal and the type of person that attends boxing matches hopes to see lots of blood. A vicarious escape perhaps but still a throwback to the days of the gladiators in the arenas of ancient Rome.

I vaguely remember the brief interludes between rounds and the coach saying little except that I had him going to keep it up. I'll never know why he didn't advise me to quit wind milling, hesitate, step back, fake a little, and get my wind back.

On and on through round after round I kept slugging mostly at the air with sweat heavy on my body and my arms feeling like one-hundred pound weights were attached to them.

Salty sweat stung my eyes and I was gasping for breath.

Finally, it was over and I stumbled to my stool to await the decision. The coach gave me a drink of water and toweled me off and the crowd sat expectant like some huge monster waiting for a bone.

The referee and judges called it a draw and I dizzily left the ring and groped down the aisle toward the showers.

In the locker room, I felt sick to my stomach and faint, totally exhausted. Alone and naked in the showers, convulsing and weak, finally cooled my body down and felt better.

Through astonished, bleary eyes the next human being I saw was my recent opponent who came to shake my wet hand and tell me how I had forced him to fight my kind of fight. And acting just like I had done this sort of thing before! I was too tired to do anything but nod my head and wish him well.

The following week I won my fight in another neighboring town but only because it bordered on a grudge fight. The reason was that this kid would go to the center of the ring, turn abruptly, run to the ropes and bounce off them, coming at me with his right arm held locked like a battering ram.

I managed to duck those onslaughts and when I caught him at the end of the second round. I battered him to the canvas. That made me feel much like the animals I had been criticizing. I hated to see this evil side of me coming out, adding further proof to the Dr. Jekyll-Mr. Hyde theory.

My next bout ended in a draw and I was pleased and surprised to realize all the fights had been in enemy camps with no cheering fans for our team. So far I hadn't been knocked off my feet and the stage was set for the County Tournament in Colfax.

To make a long story short, the County Tournament was an anti-climax. All I remember were a lot of bouts, a lot of different styles of boxing, and a lot of fear and suspense sitting out in the bleachers waiting for my bout to come up. Some old sights, sounds, and smells plus an even more blood thirsty crowd.

A kid named Tiger Lawson was featured in the bout preceding mine. The Tiger, with a half inch of stubble on his chin, was most impressive and lived up to his nickname by dispatching his opponent easily, winning by a TKO in the first round.

I was decisioned in the semi-finals and it was over at last. But what really ended my boxing career was when a new girl, Bobby Jo, from Havre. Montana, moved into town.

I'd had some thrills in the ring but there are few thrills in life that can compare to those first shy, hesitant kisses placed upon a young girl's lips. Or sweaty hands fumbling with a pair of panties and clumsy attempts at sexual intercourse in the back of a hay wagon on a moonlit night.

CHAPTER SEVEN

SUMMERS WITH THE GANDIES

Three railroads passed through our town in more or less a north to south direction. They were the Northern Pacific, the Great Northern, and the old Milwaukee Road.

From my earliest recollections, these railroads were a large part of the boyhood paradise in which my brother and I lived with our chums. Because it was the tracks themselves and the adjoining right of way that furnished us not only recreation and adventure but a constant supply of treasures also.

Spikes, tie-plates. creepers, and all kinds of discarded scrap lumber and material that wasn't fastened down we'd use to fashion into some play thing. For example, we'd collect the burned-out tips of flares and make darts out of them with the help of wing feathers from dad's white leghorns.

At first, when we were small, we'd take slingshots and shoot at old bottles or targets we'd set up beside the tracks but later, when we were of hunting age, we'd take our .22's and kill ground squirrels, song birds, and anything else that moved. I'll never forget one of these so-called "chums" wounding a stray cat, thinking it was a "bobcat" and having to crush its head with a boulder. Coyotes, squirrels, rabbits, and weasels lived in the area but not bobcats as he wanted me to believe.

Still later, when we had shotguns, we discovered that game birds, notably the Ring-Necked Pheasant and the Bob-White Quail would haunt the railbeds in search of spilled grain from the boxcars.

We'd hike for miles stalking these birds and even seek out the quail in abandoned apple orchards at dusk where they were roosting in the apple trees. If we only had a few hours after school with little time before dark, we'd take our rifles and shoot pigeons off the old Great Northern bridge nearby. More than one of these pigeons or their squabs ended up in mother's cooking pot.

Because this meat supplemented our meager food supply, perhaps this hunting was justified but I'm glad I finally outgrew my need to kill living things. It is one thing to kill to eat but to be a bloodsport trophy hunter is another.

Anyway, a few times we almost got caught on that trestle when a train was coming but managed to either get across in time or climb out onto the structure far enough to avoid being hit. At any rate, I never heard of anybody ever getting killed.

However, the Great Northern was an electric train with overhead wires and we did worry about touching the middle rail when a train was coming because someone said it was electrified.

The Northern Pacific was the line nearest our house and ran right beside our pasture which was about an acre and a half in size. I remember us always having a cow or two and some calves all the time I was growing up and we kids gave them unlikely names like Agatha or Scheherazade.

One of them got out through our rickety barbwire fence one night and was killed by the evening local. Even though it was our fault because the fence was in such disrepair. I think the railroad did pay dad $100 for the loss of the cow.

Now that I'm looking back, I realize what the railroads meant to a bunch of small town people. In reality, the trains were transporting food and materials to a post-depression nation but they also brought us a lusty, panoramic cross-section view of the human condition.

My brother and I were fascinated by this phenomenon and more than one. Saturday afternoon found us down in the "jungles" talking to the hobos. We were just grade school punks at the time playing with our slingshots but we seemed to amuse the "tramps" as we sometimes called them, and they always gave us a plate of stew or beans along about twilight when we stopped beside their cardboard shanties hidden in the high tansy.

We never knew any of their names or their faces too well either because the faces kept changing as the years came and went along with the trains. Also, in the flickering light of their cooking fires, ragged men wearing dark hats pulled low over unshaven faces all look pretty much the same.

Only one do I remember out of the thousands that must have crawled out of those boxcars to appear in our town. That day from out in back of our cellar I could look down from our poplar grove and see him walking along the track.

Then he cut beside our pasture, being careful not to trespass, moving out and around our chicken houses and up to the front door.

We had all seen these "knights of the open road" before, tramps coming off the Inland Empire highway or the tracks willing to do some odd job for a meal. In those days, many of them weren't panhandlers but would knock on doors offering to sell their goods or services. Some carried little grinders for tool sharpening.

But somehow this one was special to me. He carried nothing except a bedroll wrapped in a black blanket or maybe it was an overcoat and wore a beat-up gray Stetson with the brim pulled up.

Maybe that was it. The brim was pulled up as if he had nothing to hide or was it just because he was so proud of his smiling Irish eyes? Only God knew what was wrapped inside his bundle.

Even though I was always shy around strangers and kept out of sight behind the outbuildings, I liked this grinning, handsome man right off.

Dad was at work down at the pea processing plant and mother and I were home alone. It was a miserably hot day; my brother and sister were gone and as usual I had been off in some cool corner in an upstairs bedroom reading some hair-raising adventure story.

Mother must have been afraid of this man but she told me later it wasn't fear as much as shame because all she had to give him was some bread, cabbage, and lots of Agatha's fresh milk. He was willing to work for even that so she set about having him do some outside chores.

The strange thing was he didn't even wait for mother to cook the cabbage, just ate the pieces raw. I wondered if I'd ever be that hungry as I sat there in the woodshed and watched him split up some tough old chunks of cottonwood while he grinned down at me.

He would sing, whistle, recite poetry and proverbs and the hero-worship in my eyes must have been obvious. I guess I really needed a hero about then; a flesh and blood swashbuckler to delight the heart of a lonely bookworm.

This one filled the bill perfectly and he was magnificent standing there in his sweat and rags; confident, undefeated, proud but not too proud to do hard manual labor. Probably between 30 and 40 years old and with those muscular arms, that tousled hair, to me he was the symbol of Adventure, the Open Road. and everything I believed waited for me outside our small world. Because someday I wanted to hike off with a bedroll and some old Stetson, too. When he left, he bowed from the waist like a true gentleman, snook my hand like I was a grown man and wished me well. He tripped his hat to mother, whistled to himself as he went out the back gate and I never saw him again.

But this story is about gandy dancers and how I came to spend my summers with them. And all this because of my first real job which was as a section hand for the Palouse and Lewiston Branch of the Northern Pacific Railway back in the summer of 1947.

Before that the only jobs I had were, cleaning chicken houses, odd jobs for the neighbors, and mowing lawns. Of course I had to help dad in his garden because he loved to see things grow and with about an acre of vegetables, it was too much for him to handle alone. He always paid my brother and I for this as he did when we helped him dig ditches to run the water mains and later a cesspool.

Anyway, I was just 16, very physically undeveloped and the idea that I was expected to leave home and do a man's work at that stage in my life now seems ridiculous to me. Of course most of the mundane chores done by people in the world today are equally as ridiculous and I know that now so I can look back with laughter.

If this essay means anything it means that doing hard physical labor for a living is now stupid because we have machines for that sort of thing. There is more to life than hard work and if modern man needs exercise, he should engage in some enjoyable and strenuous sport. However, perhaps I should be grateful the railroad job took up enough of my time to prevent my becoming a juvenile delinquent.

Anyway, it was because of this job that I grew into manhood with hard muscles and a social security number. I still carry the card as a yellowed reminder but I've filled out so many job applications leading to flunky dead end jobs that I've memorized the number. On the back is typed "Section Laborer-Track Maintenance" and other data.

Not all of my memories of growing up beside the tracks are good ones and one such comes flooding back to me now. It must have happened during the winter before I started the section hand job.

That was the night my father, who had been a night marshall and later a deputy, got a call from the station master, a dignified man named Caswell I remember dad saying something about having to go right down to the depot because something had happened. I could tell by his face this was no routine security check.

Dad didn't want me to go but after a lot of persistence on my plus plug proof that my homework was done, he let me tag along. Off on a siding in the dark shadows of a grain elevator I followed Caswell, dad, and some other deputies. They flung open the door of a boxcar and there slumped against a wall sat a dead hobo with his intestines in his lap.

Before dad pushed me back I caught a glimpse of the limp, rag-doll figure, the circles of blood and smelled the penetrating odor of cheap wine and stale cigarette smoke. I thought later the body might have belonged to one of the men I knew down in the jungle. My brother and I might have listened to his stories and laughed with him while we smoked our corncobs and drank applejack from his tin cup. The paper that week referred to the body as that of an "unidentified transient."

Anyway, according to my diary, it was an early morning in July 1947 when I looked down across our pasture to the tracks and saw the work train sitting there on a siding. I might have smelled it first, though, because the odor of cooked cabbage carries far.

The boxcars had windows and smokestacks and I knew instantly these were to be the summer homes of the "extra gangs" or "gandies." Some of the townspeople were unfriendly, even hostile toward the strangers and many a mother kept a closer watch on her daughter from that time on.

For the uninformed, a few definitions: A gandy-dancer is a railroad worker who constructs and repairs railroads often miles from his home territory. Quite often, he is not a native-born American but a Negro, Mexican, Greek, Chinese, Filipino. Italian, or German.

A section hand is a laborer who is part of a crew responsible for the maintenance of a 17 mile "section" of track and its right of way. Each crew has a foreman and a "first man."

Special projects and skilled construction work are the domain of a "bridge crew". The bridge crew's boss was a stubby man named Stubbs.

Every section has a "track inspector" and ours was a bow-legged little man who looked like a banty rooster. He wore a straw hat and pin striped overalls. His motor car was a tiny one-man rig which we narrowly missed crashing into more than once. His eyes and ears seemed to always be down on the tracks like those of some Indian listening for the white man's iron horse.

Then there are train crews, both passenger and freight men, who run the trains like the engineers, firemen, conductors, switchmen, brakemen, and porters.

In the station houses are the dispatchers, telegraphers, and the top man, the stationmaster. Finally, there are all the clerks and white-collared big shots in the administrative unit in Spokane.

Before the three summers and my railroad career was over I was to have some contact with most of these men.

A typical day on the section would start when we'd all meet down at the section house at the crack of dawn and just stand there in those funny looking Mickey Mouse steel-toed safety shoes staring at our motor car and all the tools while the foreman read off a list of the trains that were due that day plus our work orders.

The "work orders" meant we were probably going out to rework or realign a stretch of track. This meant tamping gravel under crossties with square-edged shovels til we were exhausted or blue in the face, whichever came first.

But before we did any work, we loaded necessary tools on our motor car, took our oaken water cask, and went to a wine colored building which was our "ice-house". There, we shoveled the sawdust off ice blocks and filled the cask. Not with sawdust but with the ice blocks which we horsed out with tongs, washed off, threw in the cask, added water, and left for the day.

The only thing I really remember about that cask is that everyone used a common ladle and we had a couple of men on the crew who chewed tobacco. When I was really thirsty in the middle of the day, nothing was more sickening than to feel flecks of tobacco in that water on its way down my throat to my stomach.

Good drinking water was important because it has been said there's no place hotter'n hell unless it's working between two lengths of railroad track in the middle of the summer. Of course, Death Valley would have been hotter but this was the Palouse and a hot day in the Palouse is 90 degrees Fahrenheit.

When it hit that mark, we all wanted to run and get our swimming suits and picnic baskets and drive to one of the nearby lakes like Williams, Chapman, or Liberty.

If they couldn't get out of town some way, the kids would have to settle for a skinny-dip in the creek, running through lawn–sprinklers or having hours-long fights with water pistols. Only a few rich people in town had swimming pools.

Again, according to my diary, my first day of work was June 10, 1947. We apparently didn't do much that day but on the day following we fought a fire on the roof of a warehouse at Plaza which had been started by the railroad's weed burner. On that same day a train almost hit us on a curve but we managed to back up and get to a setoff in time.

I remember following that weed burner on foot for miles with Hudson sprayers strapped on our backs extinguishing smoking ties and small fires in brush piles.

At that time a campaign was underway to rid the right of way of noxious weeds and burning them was just one of the methods used.

Sometimes, we brandished scythes and raised hell with that tyrant of the Palouse, the Canadian thistle. This meant a lot of leg scratches and rashes from plunging through wild rose bushes and nettles. Occasionally, we'd be stung by bees, wasps, or deer flies.

One of the most common plants along the tracks seemed to be the billowing banks of tansy. The garden books define it as "Tanacetum Vulgare" and it lived up to its name with its vulgar little yellow button-like flowers and stinky leaves that smelled a little like camphor.

The first man was always talking about the beneficial uses of "tansy-tea," saying it could cure pneumonia, whooping cough, or chilblains. Then he would wink and tease and say that if my girlfriend ever missed her period, all I had to do was give her a cupful of this marvelous herb and my worries would be over.

I thought about Jeannie and I knew he needn't worry himself about us. Jeannie had about as much sex drive as an ice cube, and all I wanted was to have time hurry by.

So we did a lot of different things that first month and most of it by ourselves, not really involved directly with the "gandies". We tamped ties and more ties; we realigned track on curves and straightaways, built setoffs and crossings, drove spikes and creepers, put in signs, cleaned and weeded under bridges, unloaded and hauled ties and rails. We soaked ties in creosote barrels to preserve them. We learned how to flag and use torpedoes correctly. I was earning 94 cents an hour and one two-week period minus deductions totaled $73.94.

One hot day at McCoy we loaded a flock of sheep and I had to get right in the boxcars and shove those beasts in both directions in that stifling dust and stink. But even that wasn't as bad as the night a freight hit a flock of them and they called us out to pull pieces of those animals off the track and out from, under that big eight-wheeler. God, what a smelly, bloody mess!

Dad was proud of the fact I could work and wasn't afraid of dirt. One day I was sent off by myself unloading a coal car and spent the day shovelling the black stuff in a bin.

This was even dirtier than being a "creosote bum" or unloading treated ties from a boxcar. After work, dad insisted on taking me to a restaurant for an orange drink even though I was filthy dirty and the sweat and coal dust made a slimy quarter-inch coat on my face. My hands turned the glass black. I was embarrassed and ashamed but dad wasn't.

So everything we did was hard work and without the benefit of machines. Because of this, some of the crew encouraged me to go on to college or trade school or do anything to escape this life of monotonous drudgery. One of the men said if he'd have gone to school and not spent so much time around wild bucking horses, he might have amounted to something.

My parents and some neighbors thought I should study to be a telegrapher or a brakeman or something like that but I wasn't really interested. I just wanted to grow up, graduate and leave to begin my life of Adventure.

At the time I couldn't decide whether to join The Explorer's Club, Darby's Rangers, The French Foreign Legion, or the Royal Canadian Mounted Police. Somehow I felt I'd never been tested and I wanted to be tested. I wanted to be proven brave and strong and smart and my greatest hope was to be able to save someone's life someday. I didn't know how but I fully intended to try.

I didn't want to just grow old and be like all the other old men sitting on that bench in front of the pool hall, alone with their memories, waiting for death. I vowed I'd rather be dead than "rust unburnished" and be so unimaginative as to have time to sit with a water hose and sprinkle my lawn all day. The need to travel and see the world burned in me like a terrible fire.

Nor did I want to share the first man's fate. He saw me as his apprentice and I had appreciated his trying to teach me railroading but I lost respect for him when I found out that he had no desire for self-improvement. It seems he had refused a number of times to take a foreman job because he was afraid of the little bit of paper work involved. I wondered how many people in the world had lost opportunities because they were too stupid or stubborn to learn something new or take some course to learn special skills.

One night around suppertime a freight derailed when it ran through an open switch right in the yard and we were called out to clear the siding, a crossing or two and replace some ties. I recall seeing a tramp climb out of a sidetracked train and with his bedroll and pack, he was running to catch a second freight which was slowly moving through the yards. He jumped through an open door after looking in first and shouting, "anybody in here traveling?"

It may have been against the law but no bum ever seemed to be arrested for vagrancy and I suspect the railroad detectives looked the other way with these violations. I never sat in judgment of these men who could have been thieves. drunkards, sex deviates or murderers. To me they were just wretched men in ragged clothes, living carefree lives, trying to get through the world the best way they could.

Some other experiences I remember are long hours later in the summer riding the mowing machine which always seemed to be breaking down so we spent about as long repairing it.

I remember unloading endless lines of gondola cars filled with gravel and later having to strain cranking them back closed again.

About that time a jack bin collapsed at Plaza and spilled wheat and wood all over a siding and even out onto the main line. We spent half a day shoveling up that wheat.

Once after a freakish summer storm we got a report of a cloudburst at Marshall and had to make that long ride almost to Spokane to inspect the tracks.

But the most exciting experience of all was over the Fourth of July when on a curve outside of town to the north the night local derailed, the back drivers of engine number 1881 dragged to a stop after gouging ragged splinters from the ends of five-hundred yards of redwood crossties.

Some of the rails had been broken and twisted like huge pretzels and bent spikes and tie plates lay scattered along the ground. A dozen or more boxcars had been smashed and were upended or lay strewn like some child's toys.

Amazingly, nobody had been injured but a couple of passenger trains were backed up behind the wreck and the passengers had to be bussed to their destinations.

We didn't see all the destruction at first because we were called out in the dark of the night of the 3rd, destined to work all night and all the next two days cleaning up the wreckage.

The first priority was to get the engine back on the track. I was the smallest member of the crew and probably the most naive but certainly the most adventuresome so I was sent beneath the drivers to set the frogs and camelbacks in place. They sent a tiny Filipino to help me.

I shall never forget that engine rocking back and forth over me while a trainman in his starched, clean uniform with black tie, white shirt and railroad oxfords held his lantern down and whispered, "for God's sakes, boy, be careful!" I knew he just didn't want a big lawsuit against the railroad.

In the morning a railroad crane, mounted on a flatcar and called "the big hook" was brought out from Spokane or maybe it was Marshall, to disentangle the smashed boxcars.

Section crews all up and down the line were called out before dawn to start clearing away the rubble. Even more help was needed so by the time it was daylight another extra gang working in Montana was on its way to the derailment.

That was my first chance to really see the gandies in action as they busily swarmed over that wreckage with rail tongs and tie grips. When I saw the short Filipino again with a spike maul in each hand tirelessly moving behind his spike setter I thought of John Henry, the steel driving man, and his race against a machine.

Clear into the night we worked exhausted but making progress. Probably somebody brought us food but I can't remember eating anything.

I do know we got paid time and a half for overtime and double time for working on the Fourth of July itself. When we finally finished we all got to take a day off to rest up.

The rest of the summer was quite uneventful after that and I went back to school in September. I did work some weekends that winter and I'd be called out sometimes to help sweep the snow off crossings and oil the switches along with other general maintenance.

Once I was almost called out of class because of a collision between a train and a car. It seems a woman and her two little boys were hit at a blind crossing and the car and bodies were practically disintegrated.

For some reason I didn't go but the mission was to find the woman's expensive diamond ring which was somewhere in that mass of metal, glass and gore scattered for three-hundred yards along the right of way. I thought about those pieces of sheep and was glad when they called me back and said I didn't have to go especially since I knew that woman and her kids.

On January 9, 1948, Caswell, the kindly old stationmaster, died. I worked for the railroad the following summer and had many of the same experiences but only occasionally worked on large alignment or construction projects with the gandies. And I never did hear of such a thing as a "gandie-dancer's ball".

But it was during that second summer that I first saw it, a tie-tamping machine operated by one man and slowly stomping down on those ties doing the work of dozens of men. Later. I saw it again, rumbling its cage like frame down the tracks near Spangle. It was the end of an era.

CHAPTER EIGHT

A RANDOM HARVEST

Thus far, this book has been about everything except the one thing all our lives revolved around. That one thing was WHEAT! Because prosperity and well-being depended on a good crop, the merchants and other nonfarming souls like we town folk were also involved.

Therefore, even we were affected by temperatures, rainfall, bushels per acre, price per, bushel and other nonsense for purely economic reasons.

In early days, the settlers raised cattle, hogs, horses, and a lot of fruits, vegetables and even other grain crops like oats and barley but somehow wheat eventually became the victor.

The soil had always been fertile and I remember as a little kid in grade school the County Agent coming into class telling us about soil erosion and ways to prevent the twelve feet of rich topsoil from being washed off the rolling hilltops into the creeks. But every winter it rained and some of the topsoil washed away all the same.

Later in high school all we boys had to be members of the Future Farmers of America although a lot of us knew we'd never he farmers. To be a farmer one had to get his hands on a lot of good land. About the only way to do that was have lots of money to buy it or else marry some farmer's daughter. This did happen occasionally but not to dad or either of us boys.

It always seemed to me that this one-crop situation led to a subtle form of tyranny because land meant wheat and wheat meant money and money meant power. Many a Cadillac was seen driving through the fields or around town with bales of wheat straw or sacks of wheat sticking out of its trunk.

The farms were big, maybe as big as ten sections but they were twice that big in the Big Bend Country west of Spokane where the bunkhouses looked like hotels and the farmers used airplanes to fly over all that fine real estate. Anyway, in the Palouse, those sod-busters used to come into town on. Saturday nights and play poker in the tavern. We kids would peer in a back window of the card room and watch those big games where it was rumored it cost a hundred bucks to ante. But enough of that!

Most everybody in the community was familiar with the story of what happened to Old Charlie in the big city one time. Either my mother told me or one of dad's working friends at the warehouse but the story became a legend.

The gossip was that Old Charlie, who owned quite a few sections of prime acreage as well as a fine milking herd, was in Spokane on business one weekend. He stopped for lunch and a few beers in the cocktail lounge of the Davenport Hotel, but they refused him service.

Maybe part of the reason was because he was dressed in his ragged bib overalls and his feet were none too clean because only about an hour earlier he had been stomping around in his barnyard tending to his dairy cows.

There's something perhaps too unforgettably earthy about the smells of milk and manure.

Well, Charlie wasn't about to be pushed back into the street like some curdog even though his Lincoln Continental was double-parked. He got madder'n hell at the maitre de as well as the waitress and roared, "Now just a damn minute. I'm hungry and if you ain't going to feed me. I'll write a check and buy this hotel and the whole block it sets on including all the eats in your pantry. Then maybe I won't have to go hungry around here!"

He proceeded to pull out his checkbook and seeing he was serious, they ended up serving him, but they did place him discreetly in some strategically located dimly lit corner.

Anyway, I knew nothing about the actual mechanics of wheat farming and all my work experience had been in town helping with construction, janitorial labors, digging ditches, that butcher shop, and of course my main job of being a section hand.

I must have been sixteen because I had a driver's license and a car to go with it; a 1934 Chevy Coupe which I had taken a paint brush to and painted black with white wheels. It had cost me $245 right off a used car lot in Spokane.

I couldn't drive too well yet, so I made a down payment and took a Greyhound bus home, all without even test-driving the car. Don't think I even started the engine.

A few days later, dad was able to get away and after I told him where the car was, he signed the papers and drove the thing home. He said it "drove like a rabbit, bouncing all over the road."

It must have been in late July when we heard a knock on the door and we opened it to see my shy, sensitive assistant scoutmaster standing there in the twilight.

All of us liked him because he was quiet, unassuming and patient so even though he had religion, dad asked him in.

We were all wondering what he would want to make him drive all the way into town like that especially on a weeknight when there was no church meeting going on.

Well, he stood there in our living room and said he'd heard how I was driving now and had my own car and would I like to drive a truck to help he and his father with their wheat harvesting this season which would probably be about a 20-day run.

Now my little brother would have been the logical one to take a job like that because he had learned to drive bulk wheat trucks, tractors, and about anything that had wheels on it even if he was too young for a license.

However, that summer he had gone to Idaho to work in a Blister-Rust Camp so he wasn't available. Neither was my sister and it's just as well because the assistant scoutmaster was scared to death of girls and might have fainted.

I don't really remember what I said but I was thinking how I'd never really been away from home before for that long a time and it might be kind of exciting. I didn't even think that driving a truck would be much different than driving a car so I must have said yes.

The going rate for drivers was around 10 to 15 dollars a day plus room and board and cat drivers got as much as 25 dollars a day. There were some female truck drivers, some mighty young cat skinners and header punchers but I'll explain what a header puncher is later.

Well, I was to start as soon as possible so I got a leave of absence from the railroad the next day, packed my work clothes and left for the ranch south of town near Thornton.

I don't really remember making the drive but it was probably no more than twenty miles away and I managed to keep the car on the road most of the way.

The ranch house was neat but plainly furnished and I was ensconced in an upstairs bedroom with just me and all those pictures of Jesus looking out on all that wheatland and nothing else.

Now I've been calling it a "ranch" but a ranch implies timberlands and beef cattle and horses and cowboys but it was really a "farm" and these people were dirt farmers.

It was a small farm, actually, run by just the farmer, his wife, and son. No hired hands or kitchen help, just the four of us there to all get lonesome together.

I do vaguely remember seeing some old man helping us around there who I was never introduced to and he must have lived someplace nearby because he went home evenings. He may have been some distant relative called in to help share the header punching and cat skinning duties with the farmer.

Next morning, even before it's light, I hear a pounding on my door and the wife gets me up to come down for breakfast. The food was tasty and plentiful and after the wife said grace, we dug in, ate fast and started for the outside. It was so dark we must have carried flashlights or kerosene lanterns but I don't remember which.

Before that day was over, I began to wonder if farmers knew when to quit. Those days were so long, they'd have been smart to carry lanterns, two or three lunches, and work straight through and I'll bet some of those sodbusters did just that.

The farm lacked many of the niceties like trees and a spacious lawn but it did have machinery. They had one pickup, one old International bulk grain truck, one D-4 Caterpillar tractor, an International Harvester combine and the Massey-Harris self-propelled thresher.

My job was to truck all that loose wheat to a nearby elevator from both of the harvesters until the harvest was over or until hell froze over.

The first day must have gone well because I survived it and the only thing I did wrong was back into a gas pump and punch a hole in it, but it didn't explode or catch fire and everyone just kept smiling at me through gritted teeth.

However, on the second day, I was driving out of a field with a full load and despite all the waving and shouting they were doing at me to go around another way, I panicked and ran into a big eroded gully and tipped the truck over.

I crawled out a window while the others quickly unhooked the tractor and pulled the truck out of the ditch. Only part of the load was spilled and the vehicle wasn't damaged so I went on my way.

That night the farmer's wife and I had to shovel the spilled wheat into gunny sacks. She was too frugal to waste anything and I had to serve my penance and all because these people didn't heed that County Agents message years ago about gully erosion.

One afternoon at the elevator warehouse while I was waiting in line with the other trucks I saw a rig coming up behind me that looked like it was driving itself. I thought it was out of control but soon it stopped and I peered through the cab window and didn't see any driver.

I yanked the door open and a little boy hopped out. Well, I scolded him right then and there for driving that big cabover and said, "Hey, sonny, shouldn't you be at home with your mother? When she finds out you're driving one of these big rigs, you're going to be in a lot of trouble!"

Come to find out the kid had been driving for years and was really skilled, probably born in a truck, but I suggested he fix himself up some kind of a periscope so he could see out the windshield and over the hood.

I still saw it as a form of exploitation but nobody ever mentioned Child Labor Law violations and after that day I noticed other young kids driving. Some of them were girls which made it pretty exciting. Anyway, I thought that kid was probably getting paid something for his efforts but I'll bet it wasn't the going rate.

Of course there was the possibility he was another farmer's son who would one day inherit a massive wheat ranch and that would explain why he ignored me. I shouldn't have been so hasty. Maybe he'd have later adopted me.

Thus fortunes were handed down from father to son to grandson, the rich got richer, and inheritance taxes didn't appear to make much difference. At the time it seemed unfair to keep all that wealth in one family but since then I've learned to live with these basic ideas of capitalistic monopolies, private ownership, and free enterprise.

About then, that mysterious old hired hand came down with a summer flu and somebody decided I'd substitute for him temporarily in tending the header. Header punchers came in all sizes, sexes, and ages but not too many were female because the dust and the chaff blowing in the wind was terribly itchy. Unless a girl was tough and ugly, she usually preferred to drive truck or cook for the crews.

Header punchers ran all the machinery on the threshers and received hand signals from the cat skinners. A vertical bar controlled the leveling device and a sailing ship type wheel raised or lowered the swather. Another engine regulated the speed of the draper which was just a continuous belt of canvas designed to pull the wheat stalks into the thresher.

Many punchers tried to resemble swashbuckling sea captains, looking all dirty and grizzled, twisting that wheel, chewing tobacco and spitting the juice over the side onto the moving draper.

I picked up all the other skills fast enough but not the tobacco chewing part of it. I was really trying to turn that draper brown all in one day when I made the fatal mistake of swallowing a wad of Beech-Nut. The world started reeling to and fro and only a hardy pull from the water jug saved me.

Everything went smoothly for awhile until fifteen days later on a 90 degree day and with the harvest almost over. I was back driving truck that day and pulled out of the elevator after unloading when the end of my front bumper hooked an elevator door and pulled it off its hinges.

Once again, the truck wasn't damaged and the farmer had told me I'd be in trouble if I was late just one more time getting back so I decided to not even stop. The warehousemen ran after me shaking their fists, wanting me to fix the door for them, I surmised from their yelling. They told me if I wasn't more careful, they wouldn't let me come in there any more.

Well, I gave them a suggestive gesture with the middle finger of my left hand and drove on, feeling only slightly remorseful but ten or eleven miles farther on, I heard a loud bang and discovered I had a blowout.

It was the inside left rear dual and I really sweated getting it off, the spare put on and the outside dual likewise installed. Then I tried unsuccessfully to get the blown-out tire back in its holder beneath the truck.

I even tried to horse it up and over the racks into the bed but I just didn't have enough muscle and the sun kept beating down.

I finally opened the door on the passenger side and rolled the thing up over the running board and into the cab with me.

And all this trouble because I had been a little disrespectful to some elevator men.

As I approached the farm, I could look up on the hill and see both harvesters sitting motionless. I knew their tanks were full and the whole operation had shut down, completely dependent on me, the farmer's only driver with his only grain truck. I felt like God but despite the blurry world I was viewing through the rising heat waves and my stinging, salt-sweat covered eyes, I knew my duty.

Naturally, I was in a hurry trying to make up for lost time, and while rushing to load up again, I accidentally backed into the spout of the self-propelled, punched a hole in it and spilled more wheat.

The farmer bit his lip, holding in his temper, fighting for self-control and I could see the devil in the man struggling to get the upper hand. It is to that man's everlasting credit that his religion won out and he didn't kill me on the spot.

That's what religion can do for a person because I knew he was also greedy enough to be thinking about the expense in terms of parts, downtime, and labor this untimely breakdown would cost him.

Forgetting the self-propelled for the time being, they decided to load the truck "on-the-go" from the other harvester.

They had me stay in the truck and center the bed under the spout of the combine. I was supposed to watch that spout through the back window and keep it centered over the bed while both rigs moved together and the tank emptied.

We all should have known better, especially the farmer, who had decided to sit in the cab with me so the two of us could have a little man-to-man discussion.

Soon I felt the front wheels of the truck hit another of those gullies and I killed the engine. Somehow the tractor man didn't notice and the combine kept moving. Instantly. Wheat was hitting the racks, the cab roof, pouring into the open window, filling up the floorboards, the farmer's lap, and even into his eyes and mouth.

Before he got the window up, that man let loose with a lot of really foul words which I'm sure his family had never heard before and neither had I.

The day had been a comedy of errors and I had made most of them but we cleaned the wheat out of the cab and I left for the elevator while the others took the self-propelled to the machine shop to start repairing it.

Later that night I had a pretty good idea what was coming when I heard a knock on my door and it was the farmer's wife again. I knew she wasn't calling me downstairs for a late evening snack or a Bible reading or anything like that.

In her hand was a checkbook and I knew I was about to get my severance pay and my walking papers at the same time.

As she started to make out the check, we both heard a thumping on the stairs and the farmer and his son burst in yelling that a neighbor's wheat field was on fire.

Well, we grabbed shovels and wet, stinking gunny sacks, jumped into the pickup, drove two miles, and fought that fire for two nights and a day before it burned itself out.

I was so dead tired when I stumbled out of the pickup. I trudged back up those stairs and fell asleep on the bed with my clothes on. When I woke up, I didn't even take a shower, just glanced quickly at my smoke-blackened face in the mirror, reached into the bureau drawer where the farmer's wife had put my check, put it in my pocket, and grabbed my clothes out of the drawers and closet. Once downstairs again, I climbed into my car without saying goodbye and without looking back.

It had been for me the most random and wild of harvests and it was good to be back on the railroad again two days later.

CHAPTER NINE

FUNNY NORMAN AND THE MOUSE GAME

Indian summers always nostalgically remind me of one particular autumn in the Palouse hills with Funny Norman and Old Number 13.

Old Number 13 was not a football player, a locomotive, or types of whiskey, tobacco or perfume, He was a mouse.

Before I relate the remarkable tale of this rodent, I must first describe Funny Norman and explain how he and I got involved with a mouse in the first place.

With acne-covered cheeks and a cowlick hiding the rest of his Neanderthal that features, Funny Norman drifted into town in the late Thirties about the beginning of my second year in grade school. He said his name was Norman Rutledge but he soon lived up to the new handle we tagged onto him.

Probably the most unpopular kid in school, he was an orphan and stayed with foster parents who were my dad's best friends. Therefore, I felt obligated to befriend him and was terribly impressed by an orphan because I had never known one before.

The fact he was an outrageous liar and bully was beside the point. It was his shadowy past spent in faraway places that fascinated me.

Strangers in those wheat towns have to prove themselves with their fists and Funny Norman had no problem in that department because he loved to fight. Older and bigger than most of us on account of flunking so many grades, he whipped us regularly.

Now Funny Norman wasn't a hit funny because he had the aggressive personality of a wolverine with unparalleled grit. For it was he who daringly took us one at a time beneath the stage in the gym so we could peer through a crack and gawk at the girls taking their showers.

One of the reasons we called him "funny" was that his last name was always changing. We finally learned why. It was because he corresponded with some woman back east that was his favorite foster mother and her last name kept changing because she kept remarrying. I know this for a fact because he showed me one of her letters.

Despite this one truth, he was an outrageous liar because he told us once he fell out of a '36 Ford Coupe going at 100 miles an hour and it didn't even hurt him. Most cars couldn't even go that fast then so the guys all laughed at him and he hated them all. All except me. He liked me because I was a listener and fifty pounds lighter than he was.

The creepiest thing about Funny Norman, though, was his right hand. The middle finger had been broken and set improperly so it had a permanent crook in it. To shake hands with him gave us the shivers and he always wanted to shake hands.

Despite his ugliness Funny Norman was envied by the guys because his dancing ability made him popular with the girls. We noticed at the proms how he would grab some cute girl with that right hand, put a knee between her legs and go spinning off with his cowlick flying.

When the music stopped, he'd take the girl back to the sidelines and just sort of hold her hand and scratch her palm with that crooked finger.

He said that got the girls all excited and he claimed to know all about the female "exotic" zones. How we did worship him for that!

Let me digress now to say that every fall the town had a harvest festival with a traveling carnival with sideshows, rides, fortune tellers, freaks, and all that stuff.

Everybody in town got in on it. Along with these "carnies", the towns-people had booths of all kinds like cakewalks, dart throws and various other games of skill and chance.

One of the most popular of these was called "The Mouse Game". I can't recall the sponsor but it must have been one of the civic organizations such as the Active Club, the Alpha Club or some lodge. I know it wasn't a church because the churches had the bingo monopoly.

The game was similar to roulette and played with a big sheet of plywood with holes in it numbered from 1 to 100. The holes were in a large circle and each hole had a removable tin can be fastened under it. A cone-shaped cage was mounted in the middle of the plywood. The whole thing looked a little like a dart board and the bright red numbers were on the edge separated from the holes by a wire-screen fence about a foot high.

Each player had to pick a number. One mouse at a time was put in the cage and released. The person that picked the number of the hole the mouse went down won a prize.

Of course the cheap prizes were nothing and the real action was when the green folding stuff would come out into the open and he placed not only on the board but inside bets also. On a good night the betting got hot and heavy and it was strange that in a conservative town like that The Mouse Game was allowed while lotteries and horse racing were considered illegal gambling activities.

Bill Harrah and all the other pros in Reno and Las Vegas would have drooled at the sight of those rubes betting their paychecks on some mouse.

Which brings me to one of the problems of the game. That was mice. There had to be a big supply of them because some were always getting loose.

The crowd always enjoyed this because despite all that hubbub one could occasionally hear some woman scream and climb on a chair because she was afraid some mouse would run up her leg. Of course, everyone knows mice don't run up legs.

Anyway, gigantic tom cats skulked around outside just to take care of the "escapees".

Well, that year Funny Norman conned our teachers and the principal into letting he and I skip classes one entire day to go out and bring back a supply of mice for the festival which was a week away. Indian summer ended early that year because the weather turned sour.

How well I remember setting out on that slate-gray morning in early November with Funny Norman's old Model T loaded with empty gunny sacks and one or two rodent cages stolen from the Science Department. The sun coming up on the rim of the hill looked like an egg yolk floating in a glass of buttermilk.

Across frozen fields we traipsed to abandoned ranch houses and barns stalking our quarry. We found them too, but they scurried away from us and by the time night fell and it started snowing, we admitted defeat and returned to the car without any mice.

On the way back, some guy in a Dynaflow hit us from behind and sent us flying off the road across a ditch and into a haystack. It's a wonder we weren't killed but that was a typical outing with Funny Norman.

I was glad to get home that night because I had about all the bossing and obnoxiousness I could stand from Funny Norman fur one day.

It could have been worse, though, because he later told me he was able to fix his broken left rear wheel for only fifty cents.

A few days later, however. when Funny Norman and I were playing strip poker in his garage with a couple of neighborhood girls, we all heard a rustling noise behind some boxes and that's how we found Old Number 13.

Only he wasn't named that then. He was just a starving, half-dead mouse with a piece out of his right ear and a bent tail which reminded me of Funny Norman's middle finger.

We figured Old Number 13 had a recent encounter with a cat because he was a bloody mess and Funny Norman and I decided to try to save him.

We ended up taking him to a horse doctor in a neighboring town who gave him a shot and some medicine which snapped him out of it.

Old Number 13 was just about recovered when Funny Norman got the idea which would make us sure winners in The Mouse Game. He built his awe miniature mouse board designed for our pet alone.

Instead of 1 to 100. Funny Norman made his plywood sheet with a number 13 hole on it and several unnumbered holes. Then he'd release the mouse and when it went down number 13. he'd give him a sunflower seed. When the mouse went down any other hole, Funny Norman would reach in and thump him good with a ruler.

Night and day we worked with that mouse until 13 was the only hole he'd go down. Funny Norman and I figured 13 was the best number because we'd noticed how superstitious everybody was in past years and would never bet on that number.

Finally came the weekend of the carnival and it's hard to describe all the emotion, drama and interaction that was going on.

The Mouse Game was scheduled for 8 o'clock on Saturday night but the festival had been going on since Friday noon.

Let me tell now about my younger brother's part in this story. Never trusting to chance, he believed in skill and skill alone. He was an expert with darts and at the baseball throw but that year his specialty was the slingshot concession. He was so good he had won most of the prizes by Saturday noon and the guys running the booth practically threatened his life to get him to go away.

Now, my brother had this girl he wanted to impress and the grand prize was a giant panda bear. Negotiations were made and it was agreed my brother would return at eight that night to try for the panda.

I was sorry for the postponement because I wanted to see his performance but I knew Funny Norman and I would be too involved with The Mouse Game to get away.

When Funny Norman and I got to the gym with Old Number 13 smuggled away in a shoebox. all the booths were in full swing. The ring toss and the fish pond concessions were pulling in the suckers while outside the ferris wheels and the bumper cars were doing a booming business.

There were zoo animals around, too, such as an elephant, tigers, a gorilla, zebras. snakes, and birds. They had trained horses and trick riders. I can't think of much they didn't have.

The barkers were plugging the sideshow freaks and my stomach about flipped when I walked into a tent and saw a man holding a pin-headed woman in the palm of his hand. She was about eighteen inches tall with beady eyes like Old Number 13 and a squeaky voice to match.

There was a fire eater, a sword swallower, and a tattooed man. In the fortune teller's tent, I saw a dark lady bent over a crystal ball. She wore a shawl over her shoulders, a bandanna on her head and in her ears, jangly golden earrings.

I start to walk out while she's mumbling some mumbo jumbo but she grabs my hand and sits me down, saying she'll tell my fortune if I'll cross her palm with "ze silvair".

I throw some change on the table and soon she reads my palm and makes me drink some bitter tea. After that, she looks at the tea leaves and says I'm going to take a trip and meet a girl. She's right about that because sure enough that spring I am in Tumwater visiting relatives when I meet this girl.

Well, that little nymphomaniac takes me for a walk under the bridge back of the Olympia Brewery and tries to seduce me. Pushes me right over a log while we're sitting by the water. But I get her off me real fast, get up and run like hell back to the house.

That's how I almost lost my virginity and I still think about it every time I drink a bottle or can of Oly and that horseshoe with the bridge and the Deshutes River on it.

Anyway, then the fortune teller starts shuffling cards like crazy, jumps back in alarmed when I pick one and she says someone I know is going to die. I'm having too much fun to take her seriously so I put it out of my mind and walk out of her tent.

Anyway, at about 7:30, they started setting things up for The Mouse Game and Funny Norman and I crept backstage to where they kept the cage full of mice. We never did find out who got the mice that year or where they came from but they were beauties, all sleek and alert.

Some guy was guarding the cage to prevent anyone from letting them out which had happened a few times in previous years. While I explained to the guard we had more mice to contribute, Funny Norman quickly slipped open the cage and dumped in Old Number 13.

We went back out into the gym and the plywood game board was brought in and set on sawhorses. The tin cans and the wire fence were fastened in place and the yokels started gathering around. The cage full of mice was carried through the crowd and set under the sawhorses.

About then, I heard a commotion across the gym and I knew my brother had arrived with his entourage of little kids idolizing him for his slingshot ability.

At exactly 8 0'clock The Mouse Game started. When all the hayseeds were concentrating on the board with their money on their numbers, Funny Norman slipped under the table, opened the cage and scooped up about half the mice with his shoebox being careful not to get Old Number 13.

Funny Norman carried the box outside, walked around the block and turned most of the mice loose in an alley. He kept a few to set free on the ladies inside and those blood-curdling screams created such a distraction Funny Norman did the same thing with another shoebox full of mice.

Sure enough, this reduced the odds and soon Old Number 13 was picked out of the cage by the croupier.

Everyone laughed when they saw our mouse looking all puzzled with that piece out of his ear and that bent tail but then they didn't know how trained he was.

Funny Norman and I bought a couple of tickets on hole number 13 while everyone looked at us like we were crazy.

Well, Old Number 13 sauntered out and slowly walked clear around the board and went down number 13 as easy as you please. Funny Norman won a kewpie doll and I won an ashtray that time.

While Funny Norman put our tickets on the board on number 13 for the next go round and told the croupier double or nothing. I rushed through the crowd picking up all the side bets I could. I remember a couple for fifty bucks apiece and one for a hundred.

None of those men were willing to believe that a mouse would go down number 13 twice in a row. But he did. And he kept on doing it, over and over.

And Funny Norman and I just kept scooping greenbacks in because we not only won what we bet on 13 but also got all the money on the board from all the other numbers. Of course, we soon had our arms full of kewpie dolls and all sorts of other prizes, too.

It was getting late and the crowd must have been getting suspicious when it happened. Old Number 13 must have turned on the croupier and bit him on the return trip from the tin can to the cage in the middle of the board. He must have been mad because of no sunflower seeds.

Anyway. Old Number 13 jumped off the table and was soon lost in the crowd with the women all screaming like crazy.

Funny Norman and I looked and looked but he was nowhere to be found. We gave up and watched the rubes play awhile with other mice but their big money was in our pockets and only the cheapest jimcracks were left so it was kind of dull.

At about midnight, the carnival started to fold up and the concessions were all shutting down. The carnies were loading trucks and the street sweepers were cleaning up the mess. Shuffling along a back alley was the fortune teller and I swear the man with his arms around her looked a lot like Alan Amos who worked at the gas station.

Funny Norman and I, pockets bulging with money and our arms full of prizes, headed for the door of the gym.

On the way we met my brother with that giant panda on one arm and the most beautiful girl I'd ever seen on the other and I told him about our winnings. I bragged he was not the only one with skill and we had the dough to prove it.

Then I told him about losing Old Number 13. He winked at me and said. "Is this him?" and then he reached in his pocket and pulled out our mouse.

I could swear Old Number 13 was winking too.

We were going to enter him in The Mouse Game the following year but we were afraid the smartest of the farmers would recognize him.

Also we were a little afraid of the Mafia or the gambling syndicates stepping in because we were muscling in on their activities.

Because of these reasons, we took Old Number 13 out to that abandoned barn and turned him loose among his own kind.

Besides, we wanted to go into something with a little more class so we spent our senior year selling used cars.

Fifteen years later my mother sent me a clipping from a newspaper and I read that a Norman Rutledge had been involved in an accident and died after spending five days in a coma.

Right away I think back on what the fortune teller told me years before. But I never told anybody else, not even my mother.

I read down through the article and the gist of it is that Funny Norman had just been discharged from the Army when a WAC in a jeep hit him as he was getting off a bus in Michigan. That was just like poor accident-prone Funny Norman! Getting himself killed by a lady soldier!

Only I didn't think it was funny.

CHAPTER TEN

KILLSPORT

On a star-filled evening in the late Autumn of 1949 I put on cleats for the last time and played left guard for my high school football squad.

This is not just another football story but a nostalgic satire about competition. We all know what that is because we live today in a highly competitive, monetary society. competing in some way almost constantly throughout a great portion of our waking lives.

Many people thrive on competition, calling it necessary to achieve quality in all things, especially athletics. I react negatively to competition and this narrative explains why.

The reader might well ask what a scrawny boy growing up in a small wheat town in the rolling hills south of Spokane has to do with competition.

That isn't easy to answer because our village must have been the model for all those classic jokes about sleepy small towns.

The truth is. we really did flip coins on Saturdays to see whether we'd watch haircuts, the grocery trucks unloading or workmen pour concrete. And that hamlet was so tiny, we didn't even have a barbershop quartet, let alone one with only three singers!

We could park on the main drag, leave the keys in the ignition, walk away and know our car wouldn't be stolen. We could jaywalk across the street without even looking both ways because we knew no policeman would issue a ticket or no other automobile would be coming.

The community was sort of a western outback frontier Peyton Place and the object was to uncover more scandal about our neighbors than they could dig up about us. Trust was built up that way.

When a stranger came to town and pushed his way through the swinging doors of the only tavern, about thirty-five heads swiveled around to see who it was. Everybody would stare and whisper and soon the worst of the gossips would have him psyched out of his skull.

Consequently, few strangers moved in and civilization left us alone. It was that kind of town.

We had no golf courses, bowling alleys, motels, or swimming pools but for "cityfied" recreation we did have one theater which featured western movies on Sundays. The theater owner had a loud-speaker fixed onto his panel and he'd drive around making announcements and giving verbal previews.

In a town of only six hundred rubes. I was made to feel obligated to be a Boy Scout, a member of the DeMolay Lodge. a Future Farmer of America and Senior Class president. Naturally, I was forced to play football even if I was twenty pounds underweight.

Anyway, that star-filled night I'm referring to was the night of the big game and a hush fell over the locker room as "Old Jock Strap", the coach, gave us last minute instructions. If we won, we'd be the Eastern Division champions. If we lost, we'd get our butts kicked.

We called him "Old Jock Strap" because he was a balding, lantern-jawed ex-pro ball carrier. He always bragged a lot about his past heroics, yelled at us until he ran out of spit and was truly the type that would never hang up his old athletic supporter. The sad thing is, we've still got guys like him coaching in schools today and a lot of them have even moved up into administration.

I listened to him with one ear, ambled to a far corner near the rub-down table, retied laces for the fourth nervous time and made final adjustments to the strap of my battered helmet.

Suiting up was simple for me because most of the padding was issued to the running backs. None of us linemen were given such luxuries as rib and thigh pads, only ragged pants, cock-eyed helmets, and shoulder pads that must have been bought in 1482 for a bunch of guys built like Quasimodo. None of the crap fit me but I've already related my problems along with being so worried and scared of getting hurt that a lot of the time I had either indigestion, constipation, or diarrhea. But who wants to be called a sissy or a scaredy-cat? I didn't or I would have quit the team.

Usually there was a lot of horseplay in the locker room with guys sneaking around rubbing "red hot" liniment in each others' jock straps and a lot of jokes and kidding around. But not tonight with the championship at stake.

"Now remember," 'Old Jock Strap' was saying in conclusion. "These guys crawl into their pants just like you do. They're apt to be tough but they're not supermen. Get in there and fight! Win the glory for the school! The victory will be yours, not mine!"

Same old canned speech. The big sonofabitch wasn't fooling me. He wanted us to win because he wanted to be hired next year. I suspected he was bribed more than once by wealthy sodbusters who wanted their sons to be football stars.

I shudder to think of the evils that must have been perpetrated in that spoils system but maybe a small-town coach has to play politics to keep his job.

The farmer's sons were usually the ball carriers and competed against each other for the best looking cheerleaders. The captain and the fullback were both trying to lay the left halfback's sister.

I only played because they needed flunkeys to fill out the team and also because "Old Jock Strap" wasn't taking any chances on me not being allowed to play if I wanted to. I had too much on him.

Over the past four years I'd caught him behind the stage more than once with that red, haired Home Ec teacher in his arms; three times with his hand inside her dress.

"Old Jock Strap" was an egomaniac and wanted a winning team above all else to enhance his own image. He cared nothing about the overweight guys or the runts like myself and thought girls were fit only for the Pep Squad.

All of us needed a balanced program of physical education but all that bastard could see was competing and winning. Also, perhaps because of a lack of more sophisticated activities, athletic rivalry was keen in those small towns. Therefore, winning teams often had to also win the mob brawls that followed games. Fist fights were common and referees and umpires in all sports were frequently smuggled off the field or out of locker rooms in equipment hags for their own protection.

Anyway. we bound up the physical injuries and mental agonies of previous contests. wrapped our ankles and one by one jogged out of the locker room.

There were only twenty-two of us eligible for football. Most of the girls were bigger than the boys but girls weren't allowed to play football in those days.

We were actually a lousy team but that night we were expected to win because scarlet fever had broken out in Miles City and that meant they might not have some of their first string and probably a small rooting section. As if that would make a difference.

Our oversized figures cast distorted shadows on fences and buildings as we moved on past the schoolhouse and out into the streets. Our destination was the ball park that lay about a mile across town down by the slaughter house. In the dim light, the schoolhouse looked like a medieval castle and it seemed incredible that over two hundred kids were matriculated in that ancient relic.

It was a gorgeous night and a blood red moon shone the way as we pounded through the thoroughfare. The last wheat had been hauled to the elevators and harvest was over. Leaves were smouldering on backyard trash piles and the odor of them mingled with the smell of burning wheat stubble.

Since we lived in the heart of the breadbasket of the world, we talked wheat, dreamed wheat, breathed wheat dust and even ate cracked wheat for cereal. And they got 35 bushels of the crap to an acre. I got so I couldn't stand the sight of a slice of bread.

The warehouses were full of the damn stuff and it was even piled outside on the ground because the government had started paying subsidies for those guys to grow wheat. Later, they were paid not to raise it and I remember some of those moldy piles catching fire from spontaneous combustion after summer rains.

My father sweated his way up among his fellows to finally become foreman of a grain processing plant. Thousands of bushels of wheat and dry peas were boxcared out of this plant to Russia during and after the Second World War.

Some of those rich old farmers owned lots of fertile wheat land but that is discussed more fully in another chapter (See "A Random Harvest"). However, the competition for world trade and the economics of wheat is another ball game.

From out of the darkness we approached the lighted store fronts that lay on the mainstrip which was the only strip. It was Harvest Festival time and the town was engulfed in a giddy spirit.

A carnival was running concessions on a dingy sidestreet and a barker was plugging the attractions while music poured out of a noisy caliope. From the bandstand some cowboy singer was crooning "My Bucket's Got A Hole In It." (And I Can't Buy No Beer).

Shops and cafes, usually closed by six every day, had their shops open for business and one of the storekeepers yelled, "give ern hell, kids," as we passed.

Cars lined the streets and alleys, strangers wandered about wide-eyed and I knew people had come from all over the Palouse to attend the celebration.

Before I forget, I've got to elaborate some about this girl, Jeannie. It's not that she was a special girl or anything like that but people thought we fit good together.

In small towns, there always seems to be some invisible force trying to marry the men off. The home guard hated to see young guys grow up, graduate, and leave town. A lot of them stayed but I knew this life wasn't for me.

I was really shy around girls but I did kiss Jeannie a couple of times. Once when we were dancing I copped a feel or two but I was afraid to try anything else and it wasn't just because her father was one of the town marshalls.

Her teeth were crooked and she had a flat nose but I was no prize either, a dishwater blond squirt with fingernails bitten down to the quick.

I planned to drive her around after the game, maybe get somebody to buy us some beer. I'd just bought this little black '34 Chevy Coupe so I thought maybe I'd take her to the festival dance. Hopefully, she'd be willing to just go out and park and neck someplace. It sure would save me some money.

I worried a lot about venereal disease and getting a girl in trouble because if a girl got pregnant, the boy was expected to "do the right thing and marry her.

It was stupid for me to worry because I was almost a virgin and usually the girls that got knocked up ran around with the husky, rich. good-looking guys. I knew I couldn't compete with them so I ended up with the fat, skinny and homely types. I was even too naive to know how to go about laying Pearl, the town punchboard.

The sounds of hurrying peasants, chattering children and the whistles and squeals of teenagers roused me from my reverie and provided an unreal bustle to the atmosphere.

It was a great night for football and the whole town was expected to turn out to watch us perform. The air was fragrant and crisp, even cold. There might be cramped leg muscles so we were all wearing those long wool socks, especially good for absorbing blood. To me, this was just all in the game, blood and all.

Thusly. we jogged through town and onto a gridiron surrounded by loyal supporters, a lot of them old grads and assorted hanger-oners. I felt good and I'd be lying if I said I didn't want to taste the sweet grapes of victory.

The field looked to be in great shape, grass green and clipped. At least it hadn't been fertilized with steer manure like that field in Latah we played on earlier that season. Those shower rooms smelled so bad we couldn't stand to be near each other after that contest. No, the only trouble with our field was that it doubled as a baseball field and had big bare patches where the bases and infield were. Real mudholes after a rain.

The game began and from the start it was obvious the Miles City Beavers were outgunned. This surprised us because we hadn't been able to beat them for eighty years but we were told that some of their first string was out with injuries.

Nowadays, all teams have offensive and defensive squads but we didn't have enough manpower for that. Neither did any of the other smalltown teams so unless a guy goofed up bad or got hurt he played the whole game.

Again and again, we pushed them back or held because we were so frenzied, we wouldn't give the buggers an inch of yardage if we could help it. I remember Butch Hollister, our hulking center, bellowing. "Push em clear back to China!"

A white football was used, the crowd screamed for blood and the grass was already wet with dew. The band blared away. We didn't have seventy-six trombones but one booming bass drum at least. The field lights made everything as bright as day. Delicious whiffs of hot coffee and hamburgers floated across the field from the little stand nearby, a moneymaking enterprise of the Active Club probably.

I was running left guard and on end runs. I'd pull out of the line as the ball was snapped and try to get around end for some downfield blocking. In the first quarter I caught a fumble on a faulty kickoff. I ended up with twenty-one bodies on my back and never want to catch another fumble as long as I give.

I knew Jeannie and our parents were watching and that really excited me but most of the time a linebacker creamed me at the scrimmage line. At the beginning of the second quarter, the score was 26 to 3 in our favor. Boy, I was on Cloud Nine.

Then I thought about Christmas and the snows coming and after that, Spring and graduation and I'd be going away from this hick town, forever, never to return. All the truly good things lay ahead.

The whistle blew for the start of the first down and we ran quickly from the huddle. We were still fresh and jumped eagerly into position for the next play.

I crouched opposite the Miles City right guard. a small creep with the number "23" faded and almost torn off his jersey. The name "Smith" was printed on the back in red crayon. His teammates called him "Smitty" but to me, even then, he was just another of the thousands of Smiths that would grow up and compete with all the other Smiths and the faceless madding crowds in numerous subtle ways.

I was bigger than the little fink and had been giving him a bad roughing up in the first quarter. "Old Jock Strap" hadn't taught us anything about fair play and sportsmanship and it felt lovely to be taking some team to the cleaners. Most of the time we got tromped.

Charlie Keller, the quarterback. just then called a power play through the twenty-four hole. As happy as a lion eating a Christian. I licked my chops hungrily. The twenty-four hole was an off-tackle slash right over Smith.

Winking at the left tackle, Chuck Smollet. I crouched, my hind end down, legs spread, body balanced and head up, a credit to "Old Jock Strap's" coaching. My wink at Smollet meant we would once again double up on Smith, smear him out of the way and open up the slot for the ball carrier.

Teeth gritted, I hunkered down to hit Smith below the knees with everything I had.

"Hike ... 1 ... 2 ... 3!   Set ... 1 ... 2 ..."

The ball was snapped. Through the twenty-four hole we poured like a great tide. Twelve yards were gained on the play. It was third down and one yard to go for a first down.

Smith from Miles City staggered up from the bottom of that massive dog pile. I figured they'd take him out and maybe have to play with only ten players. But on the next play, there he was, sick-looking but in position.

During the last play of the third quarter, Charlie called a fake reverse pass play and little Mike Olson, the right end, went into the flat for a long one and snagged it behind the goal line making it our sixth touchdown.

In the last quarter, we really clicked and made long runbacks each time we got the ball. We skillfully executed quarterback sneaks. complicated pass plays and powerful line slashes. Somehow, we couldn't do anything wrong.

Little Smith was getting spooked at constantly being clobbered so he started standing back from the line a ways. This meant too many players in the Beaver's backfield and it cost them penalties. A couple of times they called a time out to let Smith get his wind back but that didn't stop Chuck and I from pounding him as hard as ever.

Then the final horn sounded. We hoisted "Old Jock Strap" to our shoulders and gathered in a big circle to cheer the Beavers, our assistant coach, our trainer, our cheerleaders, the band and even Kate, our scroungy. big-titted water girl. She was the only female who'd take the job. Two hundred pounds of ugly fat and probably the first women's liberationist.

Car motors started, headlights stabbed beams onto the field and into the adjoining darkness. The engines roared, their drivers impatiently competing for an open shot at the exits just as they do today while leaving drive in movies.

Each motorist, determination lines etched on sweating brow, aimed his vehicle closer, pressing all the others. Townspeople were drafted to help direct traffic and break up the jams.

Out on the field, the scoreboard read 46 to 6 as the two huddles dissolved. We left the gridiron. Just as the field lights went off, I discovered I had lost my helmet.

While going back to look for it, I stumbled over a motionless heap on that dew-saturate grass near the Miles City five yard line. Stars have shown down on a crumpled figure with bulging, unseeing eyes, a small, pale face turned upward. "Smitty" was dead.

CHAPTER ELEVEN

MISCELLANEOUS UNRELATED INCIDENTS AND COMMENTS

Every small town has at least one favorite son and ours had several but the most classic one was the war hero.

Seems the hero grew up with my Junior class English teacher, graduated went away to war. His plane was shot down and pancaked in a rice paddy in Japan and he and the crew were all captured.

When the war was over, the hero came back and wrote a book about his experiences. Through the efforts of our teacher, the hero, now a high ranking officer in the Air Force, was selected as a speaker for the class and came back to his hometown to drum up sales for his book.

Anyway, the man seemed at least seven feet tall, distinguished in his "pinks" with all the medals and campaign ribbons on it as he strode into our classroom that day.

He described what happened and said that he wasn't at all brave like Robert Taylor in the movies and before the Japanese started to torture him, he told them everything he knew about his airplane and his mission. Seems like he said he was flying either one of the Billy Mitchell bombers or a B-17 Flying Fortress.

He went on to say that before the interrogators started to pull out his fingernails with pliers or stick bamboo shoots up them, he got to tussling with the guards in the interrogation room and they knocked over some filing cabinets.

Out of those files tumbled all the latest blueprints on our long-range bombers including the B-29 Superfortress and other weapons. He said they knew as much about our aircraft and defenses as he did and there was no such thing as "top-secret" information.

Anyway, the hero was very modest and said he wasn't a hero at all but he and his crew waited out the war in a prison camp I guess, and he was given a lot of credit for being a good pilot and getting the men down safely.

At the end of his talk after he had answered a lot of stupid questions, the hero surprised us all by saying he knew Gregory "Pappy" Boyington, the war ace who had shot down all those enemy planes. Boyington was supposed to have been raised in Okanogan, Omak or Wenatchee or someplace like that so we thought it was really great to have two big heroes from the same state.

It was sometime after that, probably in the summer of 1947 or 1948, one of those relatively uneventful years, that I was next door talking over the back fence to my old neighbor, that it happened.

As we stood there with me watching and him weeding his garden, there came a tremendous roar and from out of the north from Spokane came this gigantic low-flying plane. It was a B-29 Superfortress and its shadow moved across the hills and fields as we gaped, the sound so deafening we couldn't hear each other speak.

We could plainly see the pilot, nose and belly gunners, so close we could almost reach up and touch them. The wings of the plane were wagging in recognition and salutation to our town.

The giant made several passes over the town and we found out later the hero was aboard and that was his way of saying hello.

We also found out later he was sealed in the cockpit and on a training flight so if the plane got into trouble the men would just have to crash with it. They took a terrible chance flying that low and probably got into trouble for this violation. It seems on one pass they almost hit the twin antennas of a ham radio operator who lived in one of the big houses on the upper east side.

Later, the hero settled in town with his parents and was the villain in an old fashioned melodrama entitled, "Bertha, the Beautiful Typewriter Girl." When the audience threw vegetables, he ate them.

Surely there is no finer place for a person to grow up than in a small town. One has to grow up before he knows that to be true. And he has to spend some time in the squalor and pollution of cities to really appreciate humble beginnings.

In small towns there are seldom traffic snarl-ups or mob scenes; no people pressure closing in to smother and stifle. On the other hand, there are enough people to prevent a feeling of remote isolation similar to what hermits in eaves might feel sometimes. And hermits sometimes go crazy from the loneliness because most people seem to become disoriented when away from human beings for long periods.

But the nicest thing about a small town is the freedom. Living on the outskirts of the village like we did, we boys had the best of both worlds. Living in our first house, the old barn, was too isolated and the place on the hill was too small. Besides, we got tired climbing up and down t at splintery boardwalk all the time. But this big house on the north end of town was perfect. A mile's walk brought us to the stores downtown but the country was just outside the door.

On the outskirts of town to the north was the community dumping grounds. It wasn't fenced or guarded like dump grounds are now. It was a free, do-it-yourself service and people just drove in on a dirt road and dumped anywhere they wanted to. Of course there was a good chance of getting a flat tire because of all the broken glass and rusty nails but that didn't stop anybody.

Sometimes a tractor would be working the stuff over or some man hired by the town would burn some of the piles but nothing was salvaged that I know about. At least no stands of junk were set up with the stuff offered for sale.

My brother and I would take our sling shots and later our .22's and shoot at rats or ground squirrels on Saturdays. But mostly we came to the dump to look for bottles.

Not rare bottles like today but beer bottles and soda pop bottles which we could turn in for deposit at the pool hall.

Some of that garbage was really filthy but it was all worth combing through because occasionally one of us would strike a real bonanza, a whole case of unbroken beer bottles, and free for the taking. I remember one time finding a whole mess of bubble gum cards showing vividly the atrocities committed by the Japanese against the Chinese before the United States entered the war.

Anyway, this bottle collecting was the major source of our income and we'd take our used, beat-up bikes with their home-made saddle-bags and those cheap wicker baskets made during the war and scour the countryside looking for redeemable bottles.

We'd carry gunny sacks and explore both sides of all the roads in all directions. The bottle deposit money enabled me to buy my 20 gauge Stevens shotgun and other fun items including a better used bicycle.

For we young boys, the creek was the focal point and the seasons of the year or the whims of the weather made no difference. The record snowfall for any December since 1898 fell on December 10, 1948. But we were messing around the water even after that snow melted after that bad winter and the spring floods practically wiped out the southwest part of town.

I remember my brother and I putting on our Boy Scout uniforms and helping a bunch of weeping housewives bail the mud and water out of their homes. It was just a lark to us then, too young to know the grief of losing home and hearth to the elements.

We would spend days walking the pastures and up and down the creek, either hunting or fishing or sometimes target shooting. My brother once brought his .22 rifle up from his hip in a snap shot and hit a mallard drake right in the head as it cleared the bank.

We also spent a lot of time shooting pigeons out of the Great Northern trestle but we stopped that when a woman a mile away from there reported finding her window pierced and a slug behind her piano.

My brother loved to make things out of wood and since we had no television to distract us, we both had lots of time to indulge ourselves in this pastime.

Of course we started with simple crafts like toy trains and boats made from mill blocks but my brother soon graduated to more complex projects and was much better with his hands than I was with mine.

I remember us making scooters out of old apple boxes, the wooden kind that are so scarce today, and a pair of roller skates. Once we tried a four-wheel cart but the wheels kept bending under our combined weight and that project failed. We did make a bike trailer or two and saddlebags, baskets, and other items for our second-hand bicycles.

Then we got into various kinds of weapons. Starting with slingshots, we elevated to rubber band pistols and rifles. The "rubber ammo" was made from old innertubes and a clothespin fastened to the end of a pistol-shaped piece of wood completed the toy.

We would take a piece of tongue and groove, shape it into a rifle, nail a crosspiece across the front, and presto, we had a crossbow! The "arrows" were made from thin strips of wood pointed at one end, notched on the other end and weighted with a nut for balance.

From elderberry branches, we made a plunger-type shooter that worked on the same principle as a blowgun except we didn't blow through it. A rubber band was used to propel the missile.

From young willow twigs, we made many a whistle by sliding half the bark off, notching the shaft, and sliding the bark back on.

Probably the simplest toy we had was the handkerchief parachute. We'd take a bandanna, tie strings to the four corners and a weight to the four strings and heave it high into the air, then watch it float gracefully back to earth.

I have a lot of vivid memories connected with the big house at the north end of town. The most distinctive characteristic about the old square gray place was the gigantic cottonwood tree out beside the south side. It had three big forks in it which we kids were always climbing in and if that tree had been hollowed out, a car could probably have driven through it.

Dad had to prune this big monster occasionally and many a Saturday I helped him saw logs and scrap lumber into cord wood with his belt-driven "bucksaw".

Farther north on the other side of the Great Northern trestle lived one of our pals and his family who ran the dairy. The kid always smelled like milk but he was husky and his teeth looked like something out of a toothpaste ad.

Anyway, we were going through this Batman and Robin thing one spring so we fixed up a rope to a rafter in one of the haybarns at the dairy and fastened a sack of grain to it. We'd swing way up and out and take turns dropping down on the hay or more often on each other.

One time I dropped down behind one of the cows and scared her so bad she kicked out and I felt a breeze blow past my ear as those hooves grazed me and my blood froze. Luckily, it was just a minor bruise.

My brother and I had to do the dishes nightly and other inside chores but what I remember mostly was helping mother can beets and tomatoes, churn butter and bottle homemade root beer.

Once my mother threw a tin can at me when we were messing around the front yard. The can hit me in the eye and the lid cut a gash through my eyebrow. But I had the last laugh because I really scared my mother. She thought she had killed me.

Another time one hot summer afternoon my brother and I got into a fist fight and stood toe to toe slugging it out on the front lawn while our mother and sister laughed at us until we both fell exhausted.

I remember that autumn when a kid I knew from another town accidentally killed his father in a hunting accident. It seems the kid was leading a pheasant and swung the gun around too far, shooting his dad right in the neck with 12 gauge shotgun pellets.

Maybe every town has its favorite son and ours was that war hero but maybe every town has its dropout bum failure also.

Ours was a guy named C.J. Calvert, probably a descendant of one of those grand old Southern families but a disgusting individual and a hard person to admire.

Many a time when dad was night marshall he had to tell "C.J." to get off streets and go home, wherever that was.

Down through the ages young people have always had wild ones in leather jackets to idolize. But nobody much idolized "C.J." He was no James Dean, Marlon Brando or Fonzie. He was just a punk in a leather jacket. cigarette dangling from snarling lips, eyes half closed, who never seemed to have a means of livelihood; just hung around the pool hall and a restaurant where the town whore, a girl named Melba Hamilton, worked as a waitress.

Melba was sort of fat and sloppy and certainly not any beauty but "C.J." liked her and maybe they deserved each other but the whole relationship seemed mostly depraved to a kid like me.

Of course "C.J." never knew who I was and I never met him either face to face but his reputation always went ahead of him just like it always does with notorious people.

"C.J." was never prominent in athletics or anything else in school and I don't know if he even attended or graduated because I was so much younger but he found another way to become infamous because the accident hit all the local papers.

It seems "C.J." was "drunk as a lord" one rainy Saturday afternoon and headed for Spokane with a pal of his in "C.J.'s" little coupe.

Coming down one of the last big hills on the old Inland Empire highway before the final approach to Spokane, "C.J." lost control of his supercharged car, skidded into a Greyhound bus, toppled it over on its side, and killed his pal in the seat beside him.

I think some of the people in the bus may have been killed also and certainly some of them were injured but "C.J." got off with hardly a scratch.

Well, they held a trial and "C.J." got sent up for a few years on a manslaughter charge. Soon after he got out I saw him with Melba in that restaurant we called The Greasy Spoon. I recall the jukebox was playing, "You Never Miss The Water" or "There Stands The Glass" or one of those good old tunes.

The two of them were sitting together in a booth quietly whispering to each Other. "C.J." had changed in a number of ways. He was fatter and his face was fuller. He had lost the sneer and wasn't the "hotshot" he once was but he still wore that same old leather jacket, the sleepy expression and the dangling cigarette from those sensual lips.

Anyway, I've always wondered if "C.J." hated himself down deep and had a subconscious death wish. Because it wasn't the hand of God that drove that coupe into that bus. And if it wasn't "C.J.'s" hand, whose hand was it?

We had a treehouse built in the poplar grove and later we dismantled it and constructed a clubhouse out of the materials with gunny sacks for sides. No girls were allowed and we spent our spare time mostly just sitting in the clubhouse reading comic books and smoking our corncobs.

Then we went crazy nuts about slingshots. We built a huge slingshot made from the innertube of a truck tire and transported it on a specially built coaster wagon. The whole outfit was kept hidden behind the clubhouse in anticipation of the day when we'd get up enough nerve to take it to the highway and knock cars off the road.

One time six or seven of us had a slingshot war, not with the cannon but with regulation slings. It's a wonder some of us didn't get hurt badly or blinded but we didn't suffer anything worse than a few bad thumps.

It was during this period that I made that shot that should be put in the Guinness Book of Records. Spotting a bird sitting on a wire so far away it was just a dot, I put a stone in my sling and let fly. That rock seemed to curve right over to the bird like the bird had some homing device or magnet attached to it. The rock fell one way and the bird another, dead of course.

I picked it up and saw it was a Willow Goldfinch, the state bird of Washington. I took the lifeless body home and kept it in a little box filled with cotton. I really felt bad about that for a long time after.

After we got shotguns, my brother and I hunted constantly for Chinese Pheasant, Bob-White quail, mallard ducks, magpies, ground squirrels, weasels. and rabbits.

Before hunting season opened in the autumn, we frequently fished for catfish and suckers but sometimes caught a turtle, a crawfish, or a frog by accident.

We would build rafts out of old lumber and swim and dive off them in the summer. The water was too muddy to see through and smelled to high heaven to us skinny-dippers. I suspect that more than one sewer emptied into it and some people living along its banks undoubtedly dumped their kitchen garbage in it in the dark of moonless summer nights.

That would explain why I found the empty shell and naked claws of a crab caught on a piece of brush in the shallows one day. Young as I was, I knew that crabs were not indigenous to eastern Washington. Crawfish, or crawdaddies, as we called them, were local, but not crabs.

They had been shipped in at great expense for someone's supper, and right after the Great Depression too, and the remains dumped into the creek.

Along with the water life mentioned above, the stream also was shared with muskrat and beaver. The slapping of a beaver's tail could really startle us swimmers, almost as much as having a water snake's eyeballs staring into our faces while skinny-dipping on a hot day. It's a helpless feeling even though we knew water snakes couldn't bite.

My brother and I were walking along the bank one day in late autumn either fishing or tending his trap lines, probably both, when we heard a loud splash upstream.

We thought it was probably a beaver because we could see that they had been working all around us. The trees were in various stages of ruin from the barely chewed to the toppled over to the sliced in twain.

We rushed to the sound of the splash, hoping for a glimpse of our friend. To our astonishment, the long snout and open jaws of a young alligator about three feet long appeared from the depths. revealing four rows of jagged teeth.

The alligator floated on top momentarily while my brother and I stared in amazement. Then it was gone, never to be seen by us again. Or by anyone else, either, to my knowledge. We rushed up and down the banks on both sides, trying to sight it again but to no avail. We stared silently at the spot for a long time, then stared at each other for a long time, wondering what we should do about it.

We told our parents first, and they nodded sagely to pacify us but they didn't really believe us. Also they knew we had both been smoking corn cobs quite heavily on occasion and probably figured we got an overdose of bad tobacco.

We told some others in town, our teachers and other acquaintances and none believed. They might have said they did, but they didn't. And who could blame them? Like the crab, the alligator was not native to that part of the world, either.

But just to make sure, my brother and I had that fact confirmed when we went, months later, to the curator of the Spokane County museum and told our story for the umpteenth time. We asked him if it was possible for an alligator to come out of the Spokane River, down Hangman Creek into Whitman County, and south down to the creek where we lived. He said no, that no alligators had ever been seen in the Spokane River.

It wasn't until recently that I solved the riddle, at least in my own mind. The alligator had to be someone's pet, placed in the creek or river and left to its own devices.

Not too long ago, baby alligators could be ordered through the mails, a practice which I abhor and hope has been abolished forever.

During one of my mean streaks on a cold snowy dark winter day, I loaded our old beat-up Daisy air rifle with kernels of wheat since I was out of bb's and shot my brother on the third finger of his left hand. Both of us were amazed to find that it was possible for a kernel of wheat to take the place of a bb as a bullet. Luckily, I didn't hit him in the eye and it was only a momentary sting.

Many people when grown up look back on dark night raids on some farmer's watermelon patch because everybody knows nothing tastes better than a stolen watermelon.

A mile or so from us on one of the nearby hills was a neighbor who had such a patch. Probably fearing the worst from us, he told my brother and I one hot afternoon to come to his field and we could have all the watermelons we could carry away in one trip.

We were too stupid to take our coaster wagon or bikes and tried to load two or three of those monsters in our arms and walk that long distance home. Of course the melons would drop and break and there was nothing to do but sit there in the middle of the road and eat what we could, throwing the rinds into the ditch while the farmer watched and roared with laughter. There must be a message about Greed here somewhere. I can't help remembering the fable about the monkey with his paw in the jar of nuts!

Following are some miscellaneous unrelated incidents that come from as far back as can remember:

Attending an air show at Geiger Field in Spokane. The day was hot and paper cups of water sold for 10 cent apiece.

Listening to the Joe Louis-Billy Conn prizefight on the radio June 19, 1946. Louis won by a knockout in the 8th round.

Going to Spokane to see mother's relatives and being kissed on the forehead by a little old lady in a wheelchair.

A Boy Scout camping trip at Bonnie Lake where a hunter's stew was wrapped in cabbage leaves and gunny sacks and baked underground all night.

Helping one of the town doctors in his office one night hold down a baby while he sewed up its forehead using only a local anesthetic.

A man performing a death-defying leap by jumping from a 100 foot ladder into a water trough in the middle of the football field.

Getting my first look at the Pacific Ocean at 16 years of age and digging for clams near Olympia.

An epileptic seizure of a member of the town's softball team as he stood in the batter's box.

Hearing the rumor about a local farmer finding a dinosaur bone while plowing his fields.

Realizing I would never be a famous musician as I labored along with the others in the 5th Grade song flute band.

Listening to dad and mother talking about going to a garage dance in Tensed on the Idaho line and seeing "drunken Indians in the middle of the road".

Visits from cousins living in Spokane and target shooting against railroad embankments using their big game rifles.

A man killed on his tractor when struck by lightning, another killed by a fall from a wheat elevator under construction and still another when his small plane crashed in a nearby cornfield.

A pet parade where I borrowed a neighbor's giant turkey as my entry. The turkey wouldn't march so I entered a litter of kittens instead which I transported in our coaster wagon.

Helping assemble a window display in a local hardware store during National Boy Scout Week.

Carrying the flag along with the Boy Scout troop at the head of the Armistice Day Parade.

Attending some donkey basketball and softball games played between members of civic organizations.

On January 11, 1947, the Harlem Globetrotters played basketball against The House of David in our gym. I forgot to get their autographs.

On February 7th of that same year, the Broadway Clowns played one of our local teams and I remember going down to the shower rooms to use the restroom and get some autographs. What I saw there scares me even yet.

On one of the benches in the dressing room sat one of the Clowns and hulking over him was our sheriff and a couple of uniformed policemen. The Clown's black face had blood on it and a dazed look was in his eyes.

I crept back upstairs but found out later the Clown was suspected of forging checks. This may have been one instance of police brutality but I don't know what resulted from that encounter. I only know I got no autographs.

Still another memory was going to see the American Freedom Train when it stopped in Spokane on April 13, 1948. I remember standing in the long lines among the thousands but never getting inside to see the displays. According to the diary, my brother and I were with some other people and the crowds were too much for us. We didn't have the patience to wait it out but went instead to see "MacBeth", performed by a group of Shakespearean road players.

The family all enjoyed the wild Mallard ducks we hatched and raised. We rigged an old sink up in the front yard for their "pond" and watched them learn to fly and swim until one day they flew away never to return.

One of the most historical miscellaneous unrelated incidents was a long loop trip with a boyfriend sleeping in barns along the way to visit the Whitman Monument outside Walla Walla. We traveled down through Lewiston, Moscow, Grangeville, the White Bird grade and even along the Salmon River just to visit the graves of famous missionaries. Marcus and Narcissa Whitman, massacred by the Cayuse Indians. But that's another story, already written about many times and many ways by historians.

CHAPTER TWELVE

THE DIVINE FLORA

The headshrinkers admit they still don't know much about dreams and a person can spend a bundle trying to have some psychiatrist explain the strange workings of the subconscious mind.

I don't know anything about dreams myself and I've always considered myself a pretty well-adjusted man but let me explain why I might have seething paranoid insecurities and pent-up hostilities.

It's because of this recurring dream that haunts me when I least expect it to. A seemingly insignificant nightmare but now that I'm in the "autumn of my middle years" I can ignore it no longer.

The problem began way back in 1948 and 1949 when I had parts in the Junior and Senior class dramatic productions. The plays were always directed by a member of the faculty and ours was Miss Elva Sneedly, an oldmaid type but a crackerjack of a play director. Nowadays, she'd be called a drama coach.

As a grade school kid, I had marveled for years at those productions. Some were light comedy. Some were heavy drama but the sight of the high schoolers who seemed like grown men and women to me, suddenly transformed into elaborate costumes, portraying different characters. delighted and fascinated me. Oh, how unreal the reality of it all seemed!

Tragedies, mysteries, and anything by Shakespeare was seldom attempted because they were believed to be too difficult for we country yokels. Therefore, comedy and light romances held sway but mistakes still happened.

As an example, my sister, one year older than I, then a sophisticated academic type, was terribly miscast as an Annie Oakley, gun-slinging cowgirl. She didn't muff a line but somehow failed to come across convincingly.

Somehow under the illusion that everyone in my family was a natural thespian, Miss Sneedly had given me a bit part as a teenager in the Junior play which was entitled "Growing Pains".

However, in the Senior play, "The Divine Flora", she gave me the unlikely role of a competitive junior advertising executive. I shared top billing with another kid who was supposed to be my partner in an attempt to promote an ordinary girl into something "divine".

Now I'd always spent a lot of my life dreaming in some corner with my nose in a book while the other kids were playing ball, driving hot rods, or in some other physical activity. I'd read everything I could get my hands on from matchbook covers, to comic books to Rudyard Kipling.

Therefore, I guess Miss Sneedly figured since I was a good reader, I'd be a good memorizer and a sure bet for one of the two longest parts. After all, a play book was just something else to read and the acting was incidental.

As I recall, I had to memorize over two-hundred fifty lines with all the appropriate action to match. It's asking quite a lot of a high school kid when he s got to keep up with his studies, do his chores at home and be a Senior Patrol Leader on Saturdays.

Also, in a small class of twenty-seven, I had to help paint sets, get costumes and run around town in the rain collecting props.

I took the play and the practices seriously but a large part of the cast didn't. Perhaps that was partly because the play was another one of those Samuel French teen-age farces, set in a Southern California patio. Some of the kids, wheat country hayseeds that they were, found this setting hard to relate to and thought the play was insipid and too saccharine-sweet.

After rehearsals, it was a common practice to chase around in high-powered cars playing tag and "chicken". Then, they'd go up to the Monument or some gravel pit or even out in a stubble field and park and neck and smoke cigarettes and drink beer. I say "they" because it was a world apart from me. That was for the rich farm kids and I stayed in with my books and model airplanes.

Even Flora, who was played by a skinny little bitch with glasses. Would show up late for rehearsal with beer and cigarettes on her breathe One bit player was too drunk to get through his lines. Perhaps I was a little jealous o! being left out of this world of irresponsibility; of high times with beer, cigarettes, and sex.

Anyway, one of the biggest challenges was helping Funny Norman drag in this gigantic horse trough which we made up as a bubbling fountain and waterfall with colored lights on the bottom.

We also took his old Model T truck and brought in all sorts of greenery and flowers which the townswomen gave us to complete the tropical look. The odor of those rain-kissed lilacs, roses, and daffodils was overpowering even if they weren't tropical.

A flight of stairs was set up in back. I mention the stairs because they have a definite meaning to the story and always appear in my recurring nightmare.

Now remembering your own dreams of being naked on a streetcar and trying to cover yourself with a newspaper which isn't big enough or falling off a cliff and never reaching bottom or being unprepared in the wrong classroom on test day without paper or pencil, you'll appreciate how dramatically real this all seemed.

In my dream those stairs and the whole patio are as vivid to me today as if I were still playing that part in "The Divine Flora" back in 1949.

Anyway, it was the matinee performance and I believe it happened in Scene Two of Act Two. The farce had gone quite well up to then even if the cast did look tired out and hung over from all their nocturnal activities after the Dress Rehearsal the night before.

The scene just rendered was one of a teen-age dance on this patio on a balmy summer evening and we boys were all dressed in white dinner jackets with carnations in our buttonholes.

Scene Two of that same act is supposed to be the prelude to a tennis game and all of us were wearing tennis whites. The dressing rooms were in reality the school's locker rooms and reached by back stairs behind the stage.

Quite a bit of action and dialogue occurs among the other players between the closing of the dance scene and the time I'm supposed to make my appearance as a tennis player.

However, this is to be my big scene because at the conclusion of it, I'm supposed to have a temper tantrum, throw down the tennis racket, and rush back up the stairs, yelling, "I'm going to sleep in the boathouse!"

But something goes wrong because I've just started to take off my trousers and dress shoes when three prop extras come rushing down those stairs yelling. "Hurry, you're on!"

"But I can't be," I protest weakly. "I've plenty of time to get changed because I don't come in for three more pages!

The stage hands explain in hysterical tones that the cast has left out those three pages.

I throw on my tennis clothes, grab my racket and charge back up the locker room stairs, and into the back of the stage.

From the top of those patio stairs I look down and hear those poor kids adlibbing. They're standing in the middle of the stage and one is saying. "When do you think Randy (that's me) will get here?"

"I don't know," says another, "but I hope it's soon."

Staring in disbelief at the white face of the prompter who is helplessly struck deaf and dumb writhing in the wings, I decide to continue as if nothing had happened and enter as if I'd hear my cue.

We limp shakily through the rest of the play but we certainly didn't receive many plaudits for that afternoon show. Fortunately. just the student body, the faculty and a few bored housewives were in the auditorium for the matinee. Unbelievably, the evening performance went without a hitch.

And that's what my recurring dream is about; amateur theatrics and a wound that never seems to heal but leaves forever a hidden bleeding scar. I always wake up at the moment I'm on those patio stairs unable to remember what my cue is or what line to recite.

It's enough to keep me from joining some little theater group in hopes of satisfying inner ego needs and releasing emotional frustrations.

CHAPTER THIRTEEN

THE END OF THE BEGINNING

The end of the beginning was that big ice-skating party at Nib's Pond we Seniors threw in the winter of 1949. We'd swept the snow off the ice, built a fire out of old tires and bribed somebody's older brother to get us some good drinking liquor.

I didn't have a date for that outing and probably would have frozen to death if it hadn't been for the fire and that good Jim Beam.

We stags could see the couples pairing off with their steadies for some petting by the fire. Jeannie wasn't there and I felt sort of odd because everybody figured the two of us were "bespoken" and would probably get married someday.

But I was too adventurous for that so J just skated around with the other unattached guys using an old heel for a hockey puck and stayed in the shadows outside the firelight, dreaming my dreams.

I'd look back across the orange glaze of frozen ice and see those boys squeezing those girls under those blankets and I sure felt left out.

But after all, I knew it wouldn't be fair to ask any woman to share my life because it would be filled with dangers and insecurities. I didn't mind suffering or maybe even getting killed in my search for Adventure but I had no right to drag any female along.

By that time I had read all the Richard Halliburton books including The Glorious Adventure, Seven League Boots, New Worlds To Conquer. and the First and Second Book of Marvels.

So even though I lived in the Palouse, my heart was on the Road to Mandalay. In my fantasies I was diving into the sacrificial Well of Death in Yucatan or swimming in the sacred pools of the Taj Mahal.

Lord, how I loved those stories and read them over and over again.

Then none too soon the Senior Play was over which I described in "The Divine Flora" and in the middle of May we had the Senior Prom.

I did have a date that night but it wasn't with Jeannie. It was with some fat girl from another town and I won't mention the name of either. I hardly remember her or the dance but I do recall the night because I had to buy a corsage and my little '34 Chevvy coupe broke down right in the middle of the Northern Pacific railroad tracks. In my best clothes I pushed the car with the fat girl inside off the tracks and had to walk a couple of miles to a gas station.

The attendant locked the station and drove me back in his tow truck and gave my car a tune-up by flashlight. Don't remember how I got the girl home but I know I never even touched her and was too embarrassed to even kiss her goodnight cause the mechanic just kept grinning and staring at us all the way back to the station.

Then came the Senior Sneak. We took all the money we had out of the class treasury and chartered a bus to Lake Christina in British Columbia.

Just before the bus was scheduled to leave the Spokane depot, the girl that was the class's valedictorian received a whispered message from the bus authorities and started crying. It seems her mother had been hit by a car right in front of the Methodist Church back home. That's all very vivid to me because they took the girl off the bus and when we got back after that long weekend, the mother had died and her dried blood was still on the pavement swarming with flies. The town hadn't even bothered to wash down the streets.

That woman's accident sort of put a damper on the whole excursion but nobody seemed to think we should cancel the trip.

With us as chaperone was our class advisor and science teacher. He had his new bride with him and she was supposed to look after the girls while enjoying her honeymoon.

Well, we were hardly out of the city limits with over two hundred miles to go when some of the guys started telling jokes, singing nasty songs, getting louder and louder With their raucous laughter. I don't think any of them smuggled any liquor on board but everybody could smell tobacco smoke coming from the last few rows of seats.

I'm left out of all this because the advisor likes me and trusts me and is counting on me to set a good example for the rest of the guys. For that reason, he hardly takes his eyes off me the whole trip. And I hardly take my eyes off his gorgeous wife.

We cross the border and stop for a break in Grand Forks. We walk around a little, buy a few trinkets and get back on the bus. Soon we're in the wilderness and eventually pull up to the lodge on the shores of Lake Christina.

The lodge owners soon have us all installed in little white cabins, the boys separated from the girls, of course, with the advisor and his bride in a cabin halfway between.

The lake is too cold for swimming and none of us have brought swimming suits anyway or any fishing gear either so with so little to do we're bound to get into trouble.

Some of the guys and one or two of the most promiscuous girls befriend some young Canadian boys that are sort of hiking through and get those boys to go to the little store near the lodge. Pretty soon the Canadians come back with a sackful of beer, cigars, and black cigarettes named "Black Cats." The girls drifted out of sight but we boys retire to our cabins and start puffing away on those strong cigarettes and swilling down the equally strong beer. Somebody has brought some playing cards so we start playing poker and are having a high old time when we hear a knock on the door and it's the advisor making bed check.

The guys quickly hide the cards and the beer, and scram out the back windows while I open the door and explain to the advisor that everything is okay and no cause to get upset. Since I can still talk without slurring too bad, he tells me to try to keep the guys under control and leaves, heading back to his cabin and his new wife.

We get the beer back up from under the floorboards and start playing cards and smoking again. By then, some of the guys are really sick and start throwing up all over the place and I'm afraid I will too so I go out for a walk.

It's while I'm walking I start thinking about the advisor and his pretty wife. Standing out under the moon I see Funny Norman, who's bunked in another cabin and like me, pretty mature for his age.

Anyway, Funny Norman and I decide we should peek through the advisor's cabin window to see if we can catch him in bed having sex with his new bride.

We climb up on old boxes outside in the dark and peer in, seeing the advisor still in his sport coat, white shirt and tie which he hasn't taken off since we got there and he's just talking to her while she's sitting on the edge of the bed.

She's got all her clothes on, too, and Funny Norman and I watch and watch but they both just sit there and keep talking. We're both getting drowsy what with all that beer and finally the light goes off and we can't see any more so we go back to our cabins and go to bed.

Next day we all get up and since there's not much else to do and we're all in our play clothes. we decide to hike up to a ridge for a view of the lake. We make a big loop trek past an old dance pavilion and some of the girls are pretty tired by the time we get back.

As I recall, there was a boat rental and I think some of the guys took their girls out on the lake in rowboats. All this time Jeannie and I had sort of been looking at each other from afar and trying to be aloof so's nobody would notice us looking at each other.

On our last day. I casually asked Jeannie if she'd like to go horseback riding with me. She said okay so we rented a couple of nags from the nearby stables and took off alone on a trail around the lake.

All day Jeannie hadn't said much, just smiled at me sweetly as we rode along and I was lost in thought myself, dreaming as always about what lay ahead for me in the future.

In the early afternoon, I spotted an abandoned houseboat pulled up on the edge of the lake. Then the thought came to me from out of nowhere like a summer squall that this was going to be the spot where Jeannie and I were both going to lose our virginity!

Jeannie might have suspected what I had in mind but if she did she kept it to herself and went along willingly when I suggested we dismount and explore the houseboat.

I shortreined the horses to a sign nailed to a tree and started down the bank, leading Jeannie by the hand.

Down the rickety stairs we went and around to the back, where I figured I could pry a window open without too much trouble.

I had just kissed her gently on the mouth and sort of felt her all over with the houseboat rising up and down in the water when we both heard a cracking sound followed by the clatter of the horses' hooves.

We both knew what happened so we let loose of each other and ran back up the stairs but it was too late. The horses were pounding out of sight down the trail and around the bend.

Those nags had torn the sign off the tree and one of them had slipped out of his bridle and it was lying there in the dust. As I picked it up I knew there would be no sexual adventures for Jeannie and I that day and all that remained was a long, long hike back to the cabins.

Well, we got back to the stables after dark and everyone was standing around grinning and staring at us and especially at me with the broken bridle in my hand. They all knew what had happened because the horses had run straight back and had been there for hours. Nobody seemed worried that we might have been hurt. The stable hands were practically laughing out loud and Jeannie was almost in tears. This was just another of my many problems with horses. I should have known better.

So my Senior Sneak ended on a shameful note for Jeannie and I. It provided some humor for the others but not enough to make up for that woman's death back home.

The real end of the school year, though, was, of course, Graduation Day preceded by the Baccalaureate sermon held the night before in that same Methodist Church with that blood on the sidewalk out front.

Anyway, the class had this big dispute over who was going to make the student speech. I think the valedictorian, the salutatorian and the football captain all made speeches but I could be wrong about the valedictorian because her mother had been killed in that accident and she was still in pretty much a depressed state of shock.

Anyway, I was Class President, a job no other stupid goon would take. and the class wanted me to present the Superintendent with a check for enough money to buy a cornerstone for a new high school. I'll never know how the class had any money left after that Sneak but I do know the Treasurer or somebody swindled some dough away from some other class. Seems we had some confetti left over from the Prom and charged the other class three times what it was worth.

When the time came. we graduates all sat like frozen dummies in that auditorium while we sweated through the ceremony and speeches. Athletic letters and awards were given and then the scholastic honors and more speeches. Finally, the diplomas were passed out.

I was up on the stage beside Jeannie who was the salutatorian and after she got up to make her speech, the Superintendent went back to the microphone and shocked me all to hell by presenting me with the Citizenship Award. If I was a good citizen, I pitied the world.

I stumbled to my feet then, accepted the award and began to make the cornerstone presentation. I said, "On behalf of the Senior Class. I'd like to present you with this check for a cornerstone for a new high school . . . uh . . . because . . . uh".

"Because you thought you should've done it!" the Superintendent finished. The crowd roared with laughter but freezing up like that so he had to help me through it was one of the most embarrassing moments of my life.

But the real end came for me just a few days before all these ceremonies and speeches when mother told me she was getting a divorce after twenty years of marriage.

That month of June was spent in hearing first mother's and then dad's side of what happened and their respective reasons for the divorce. The result was the family broke up and we all went our separate ways, never again to live in that town.

The beginning of my new beginning was when I realized that growing into manhood was a painful thing and I wasn't even there yet. I'm not sure I am now. I came to know life was a bittersweet reality, filled with tragic-comic elements.

A lot of things I learned later. I learned that growing up in a small town might be boring and limiting but maybe still better than growing up in the confines of a puke-hole city slum ghetto.

I learned that life is a compromise, that success is hard to define because everybody's got a different definition. I've never felt successful and even though I always did what was expected of me, all the "right" things, I'm still a failure in my own eyes.

Maybe that's because my boyhood dreams of a life of travel and Adventure never came true. Most of my travels were arranged for me while soldiering in the U.S. Army.

What hurts most of all is that I think I paid my dues and made an investment in myself but I don't honestly believe I received a full return on that investment, at least not yet.

But even before I decided to go away to college in September, I knew then in the Summer of 1949 I had to leave but I wasn't sure of where I was going or what I'd find when I got there.

I only knew I had to go and as Tennyson wrote, "to strive, to seek, to find, and never to yield". I'm still not there but the joy has been in the journey, the pleasure in the quest, and it's taken me all these many years to learn that. And even more years to write down on paper these words about my own life.

1949

1978

THE AUTHOR

Robert D. Easton is a native of the State of Washington. He has two liberal arts degrees from Central Washington State College at Ellensburg, Washington and has done postgraduate work at several other colleges.

A veteran of the Korean conflict, he served in Europe as well as in numerous Stateside army posts as a teletype operator and message center clerk for the U.S. Signal Corps during 1953–1954.

At various periods in his life, he has worked as a truck driver, section hand, janitor, newspaper reporter, schoolteacher, technical writer, landscape technician, parks maintenance worker, nurseryman, harvest hand, insurance salesman, and is currently a public school employee.

He was a winner in the 1974 Writer's Digest. Contest and has written non-fiction articles for Air California, National Humane Review, Horse and Rider, Sacramento Magazine, and Good Old Days Magazine. Hibiscus Press (In A Nutshell) of Sacramento. California, has published four of his short stories.

He is a member of the California Writers Club, is 47 years old, and lives in Sacramento with his wife and three daughters. This is his first book.

www.ingramcontent.com/pod-product-compliance
Lightning Source LLC
LaVergne TN
LVHW040151080526
838202LV00042B/3115